Trauma-Informed Behavioral Intervention

What Works and What Doesn't

Karyn Harvey

D1283869

ISBN: 978-1-937604-04-2

"Our lives begin to end the day we become silent about things that matter."

—Martin Luther King, Jr.

This Book is dedicated to Steve Harvey, my dear husband

Special Thanks to Daisaku Ikeda for shining the light that illuminated my life; to Merle Kougle for her exquisite assistance; to Ryan and Tara Harvey for being wonderful and patient offspring; to all my friends and co-workers who guided me with thoughts, ideas, and insights; and finally special thanks to my mother, Violet Manon.

Table of Contents

Introduction 1

1 The Solution Becomes the Problem 4

2 The Functionality of the Functional Assessment 17

3 Prevention Before Intervention 29

4 The Dangers of Misdiagnosis 35

5 Crack Babies, All Grown Up 42

6 The Truth About Trauma 51

7 Stabilization 64

8 Trauma-Informed Crisis Prevention 74

9 Trauma-Informed Crisis Intervention 83

10 Mental Health Plans 91

11 Programmatic Services From a Trauma-Informed Perspective 120

12 Stepping Into the Here and Now 126

Introduction

Why do we assume that individuals with intellectual disability (ID) who are having behavioral issues are doing so in order to gain some outcome or to manipulate someone? It is because we in the field have long adhered to a behavioral paradigm based on an applied behavioral analysis approach. Rarely do we stop to question this approach.

Recently, I was made aware of a situation in which a traditional behavioral approach was used toward a young woman who had an intellectual disability as well as a hearing impairment. She was repeatedly screaming, crying, and begging for attention. A psychologist completed a functional assessment and concluded that this individual was doing so for attention. One medical examination had been completed in which a general practitioner determined that she did not have anything physically wrong with her. She had not been referred for further testing, although she complained of pain. People without disabilities are often referred for an MRI, CAT scan, or sonogram if there is pain but no obvious cause. This was not done for this woman. The psychologist was confident in the assessment that there was no physical problem. He wrote a plan that clearly instructed staff to ignore much of the screaming. Several weeks later, the woman died, cause unknown. The autopsy was inconclusive.

This is not the first time I have witnessed such a tragedy in the field of intellectual disability. Cries for help are often interpreted as manipulations for attention; not unusually, the procedure of choice is to ignore the cries and pay attention only to "appropriate" verbalizations (Clements & Martin, 2002). Imagine if you were unable to garner appropriate medical attention, even though the system of care was available to you. Imagine if however much you complained, people ignored you and rebuked you for your complaints whenever you were addressed. Imagine if the complaint you were making turned out to be a matter of life and death.

This woman was in a state of physical trauma. The example is a harsh one, but it did occur. There are also many, many individuals with ID whose trauma is emotional. We may, in fact, be misunderstanding many behavioral issues when the core of these issues is the expression of emotional trauma, not attempts to gain a reaction. The profile of an adult with both ID and a behavior problem looks alarmingly similar to the profile of an adult with posttraumatic stress disorder (PTSD). According to Judith Herman (1997), there are three outstanding symptoms of PTSD: (a) the person feels unsafe—in cases of adults with ID, many acts of aggression occur in circumstances in which the individual feels threatened or unsafe; (b) the person feels devalued—often in the past, the feelings of individuals with ID were not taken into account, nor were they treated humanely during the trauma, and now they are carrying this feeling of not being valued or valuable with them; and (c) the person feels and appears to be disconnected from others.

I believe that these symptoms directly reflect the condition of many individuals with ID. They do not feel safe, they do not feel connected to the larger world—or, in many cases, to others at all—and they do not have power. People with ID are often the least valued, most ignored, and most vulnerable in their environment.

The *Diagnostic and Statistical Manual of Mental Disorders* (*DSM–IV–TR*; American Psychiatric Association, 2000) defines PTSD as

> the development of characteristic symptoms following exposure to an extreme traumatic stressor involving direct personal experience of an event that involves actual or threatened death or serious injury, or other threat to the physical integrity of another person, or witnessing an event that involves death, injury, or a threat to the physical integrity of another person, or learning about unexpected or violent death, serious harm or threat of death or injury experienced by a family member or close associate. The person's response to the event must involve intense fear, helplessness or horror. (American Psychiatric Association, 2000, p. 463)

Anyone who has seen Geraldo Rivera's "Willowbrook" (Primo & Rivera, 1972) exposé or known individuals who have survived long-term institutionalization will recognize that those individuals' experiences match the experiences described by the *DSM*. It is easy for those of us who work with people with ID to forget the trauma that many have endured. It is also easy for us to underestimate its impact. This impact has far-reaching repercussions, manifesting in a variety of ways that we may very well be misunderstanding.

It is possible that many of the responses of individuals with ID that we call "behavioral issues" might actually be manifestations of trauma and trauma-based responses. It is traumatic to live in this society with an intellectual disability. Further experiences of abuse, neglect, and/or invalidation compound the trauma. I contend that the manifestation of trauma and its impact can look very behavioral but might, in reality, be trauma-based responses, manifesting symptoms of PTSD.

In this book, I will first outline the ways in which individuals with ID may have actually been damaged by our "behavioral" approach to their day-to-day actions. Next, I will attempt to demonstrate what has been missed through this approach:

Needs have not been met, individuals have been misdiagnosed, and trauma responses have been triggered through the exclusive use of behavioral controls, both positive and negative. I will attempt to demonstrate the ways in which this damage has been done.

Finally, I will outline what I believe should be done instead. In Chapters 7–10, I explore the topics of stabilization, prevention, intervention, and the mental health plan. In Chapter 11 I propose a model of behavioral intervention that does not require the use of restraints or contingencies, instead promoting safety and security and addressing the outstanding issues around trauma. Many case studies will be discussed but all the names and relevant details have been altered to protect individuals, staff, and agencies.

The mental health plan template that I propose adopting instructs and informs staff about how to support people who have experienced trauma, both on a small scale and on a large one. I provide examples of this approach with actual case studies, and I illustrate how the plans should be written to ensure optimal implementation. My goal is to give the sincere professionals and paraprofessionals who have dedicated themselves to this field and to the welfare of individuals with ID a better way to support these individuals psychologically. My belief is that this requires both a different paradigm, one that is trauma informed, and a different approach, one that is based on establishing the critical elements needed for total recovery. When the individual recovers, behaviors change. When the individual recovers, happiness can begin.

References

American Psychiatric Association. (2000). *Diagnostic and statistical manual of mental disorders* (4th ed., text revision). Washington, DC: Author.

Clements, J., & Martin, N. (2002). *Assessing behaviors regarded as problematic for people with developmental disabilities.* New York: Jessica Kingsley Publishers.

Herman, J. (1997). *Trauma and recovery.* New York: Basic Books.

Primo, A. T. (Producer), & Rivera, G. (Correspondent). (1972). *Willowbrook: The last great disgrace* [Video].

The Solution Becomes the Problem

At times, in the field of psychology of intellectual disability, the solutions that we implement have actually worsened the problems. We have tended to view behavioral issues as separate from the thoughts, emotions, feelings, and experiences of the person behaving. It is simpler to do this, it makes a neat package that can be clearly addressed. ABC (antecedent, behavior, consequence) can be examined without examining the unique features of the individual (Mahoney, 2002). However, when the fundamental experience of the individual, the traumas he or she has endured and the emotions associated with those traumas, are ignored, a behavioral intervention can, at times, worsen the individual's internal condition. It can become a trigger for further traumatization.

Denny

To be left alone at 4 years old, in an institution that is filled with screaming people, smells of human neglect, and is packed with chaos, is no way to begin your preschool years. Just ask Denny. Staff, charged with 35 to 40 children, could not take care of him in any meaningful way. It was no wonder that at age 40, when he left the institution and entered a community-based agency, his actions were full of agitation, fear, and aggression.

He huddled in a corner at the day program on his first day. He threw chairs if anyone attempted to get near him. He would talk to only one person: a fellow ex-resident of the institution. He spoke only in one- or two-word sentences when he did talk. At home, he ate ravenously and put holes in the walls when staff tried to help him bathe. As the weeks went on, staff in both settings wore down his defenses and began to be able to communicate with him. He bonded with one or two and looked to them for reassurance. He still became agitated frequently, despite the large doses of Haldol in his system, and threw chairs and flipped tables at seemingly unpredictable times.

As the weeks wore on, however, he relaxed more and more. Day program staff noticed that he was most agitated around the program manager. When she entered the room, he would often start screaming and throwing objects. He broke a few ceiling panels with flying chairs. Staff urged her to stay away from him.

Enter the consulting psychologist. The director had called the psychologist to write a behavior plan for the day program. "Stop the property destruction" is the request. The psychologist observes Denny, who is holed up in a large room sectioned off by desks that encase him as he sits in a chair and mumbles incoherently.

The psychologist spends 3 min observing Denny and then interviews staff. Three weeks later, a "behavior management plan" arrives. The psychologist's assistant delivers it and trains the staff. The plan includes ignoring Denny when he mumbles, restraining him in a basket hold when he engages in property destruction, and taking him down to the floor when he attacks others. Denny gets 50 cents for a soda every day that he refrains from property destruction and aggression.

Several weeks later, the staff are busy taking Denny down to the floor, sincerely trying their best to follow the behavior management plan. Denny is screaming hysterically. He is reliving abuse that he endured in the institution, the aggression from the other institutional residents, the attacks and violent restraints by staff.

The very well-meaning staff were following what they thought the behavior management plan outlined. Denny, in the meantime, was terrified. Out of terror, he wriggled and flailed while they had him pinned. He finally gave up. The staff thought that he had calmed down and the procedure had worked. They were impressed. Meanwhile, Denny realized he could not trust the few staff members he had begun to like and withdrew further from everyone. His anxiety and fear grew and grew, and a few short days later, he directly attacked the staff. The best defense, a panicked Denny assumed, was a good offense.

Staff responded by restraining him more quickly this time, because they saw how restraining him had calmed him down earlier. Denny acquiesced quickly because he knew that these people were not safe, and he assumed that, like others in the past who had put their hands on him, they would hurt him if he tried to get away. So the cycle of fear, aggression, restraint, increased fear, increased aggression, and more restraints was strengthened. Denny became more, not less, aggressive as a result of staff's interpretation and implementation of the plan. Denny never earned the rewards outlined in the plan, and the staff, so involved in watching Denny for signs of aggression and attempting to control his outbursts, forgot to give any verbal praise.

When the team reviewed the data, they concluded that more medication was needed. So Denny's medication was increased in order to control his aggression. Denny, now more drugged, was slower to respond. However, the drugs did not allay his fears. He would lash out to defend himself against attacks he was sure would be coming, and as though to confirm his theory, staff would restrain him, only taking their time now, because Denny's responses were so much slower.

When Denny felt unsafe, because staff ordered him about or laughed at him, he would say over and over again, "I'll go off . . . I'm going to go off," as if to defend himself. Staff began to say that also and laugh. Now that Denny was more medicated, no one was afraid of him.

In the early days of community placement, this was often the scenario that resulted from behavior management. Behavior was defensive, restraints were implemented, and fear on the part of the restrained person increased. Behaviors out of fear, usually aggression, increased, and finally, the person was brought to the psychiatrist and medication was increased. I, as one of the psychologists writing the plans, was an integral and guilty part of the process.

Leslie

Sometimes medications cause nerve damage, such as tardive dyskinesia. Other times they cause impaired liver functioning and sometimes kidney damage. On rare occasions, death due to lethal interactions of medications has occurred (Tiihonen et al., 2009). Leslie required a behavior management plan as well. Both the day program and residential staff reported that she was noncompliant. She refused to do her work during the day and would not stop talking or do her chores at night. Her plan included restricting her mobility and redirecting her with verbal prompts back to the work table and the chair in which she was supposed to sit all day. This, of course, did not work. She would and could not sit for more than 10 min. By the end of the day, the staff were hoarse, and Leslie still had not sat for more than 10 min at her work seat.

The staff finally gave up, and a forward-thinking manager suggested that she receive counseling. The therapist arrived, looking to sit and talk with her and discuss the many shades of feelings she might be experiencing. Instead, Leslie refused to sit. She walked in circles while repeating phrases. The therapist realized, while being circled, that some of her phrases sounded like snatches from different languages. After several sessions of fruitless, nonsensical verbal exchanges, the therapist tried writing. Leslie became excited when she saw paper. She wanted to write letters.

The therapist shared this with the staff, who did not know that Leslie could write. Leslie began writing furiously. She sat for over 20 min, writing letter after letter. Her bob of curly white hair bounced up and down as she wrote, her spindly elbows and fingers darting back and forth with each word. When the session was winding up, the therapist asked to see the letters and discuss them. To the therapist's amazement, the letters were in French and German. When she asked Leslie how she knew all those words, Leslie replied, "I know many languages."

In the next session, the therapist requested that Leslie write in English. Leslie agreed congenially and began writing. Her letters, all written to a favorite staff member at the work site, revealed stories of growing up in a local institution for the intellectually disabled. Stories about being told "no," stories about being "bad," and disjointed stories about family members poured out of her. Then she was finished. She would write no more.

The therapist realized that Leslie preferred to be in motion. Leslie and the therapist began to go for car rides. During the car rides, the therapist saw Leslie relax for the first time. Finally, Leslie began to talk. She had been put in the institution as a young girl, she had missed her family, she had never understood why she had to be there, and she hated where she lived now in a three-person home. The staff were mean, as were the other ladies in her home, no one talked to her nicely, and she was tired of the food. Her story poured out again.

The therapist visited Leslie at home. The staff complained bitterly that Leslie never slept, never stopped, never even slowed down. The therapist arranged a consultation with a psychiatrist. Leslie was currently receiving the "cocktail for mental retardation," which included both Haldol and Mellaril with a splash of Thorazine.

The consulting psychiatrist gathered people from every area of Leslie's life. Data from her unsuccessful behavior plan were reported by day program staff; patterns in her sleep or lack of sleep were reported by house staff; the therapist reported on therapy. The psychiatrist asked many questions. Several weeks later, there appeared a thorough report, which the therapist trotted over to Leslie's prescribing psychiatrist. The report recommended addressing a schizoaffective disorder with specific medication rather than global mental retardation medication. Leslie was placed on some of the recommended medication by her prescribing psychiatrist, but the cocktail Leslie was already on was not changed. Three weeks later, Leslie was dead.

The autopsy ruled that her death was a result of a deadly medication interaction. The funeral was held, and a brother whom no one knew appeared. He was extremely distraught and told a story of Leslie being placed in the institution as a child because she did not "fit in." Institutionalization had been the doctor's recommendation.

Years later the brother reflected that Leslie had been mentally ill but never intellectually disabled. She learned to act as though she were cognitively impaired, he said. Her chronic mental illness and its early onset were more than anyone understood in the mid-1960s. She took on the identity of a mentally retarded person or client and never developed her many gifts, including her gift for language. The brother blamed himself for not speaking up, but as her younger brother, the chances were that no one would have been inclined to listen to him. If properly medicated, she might still be alive today. She also might have been able to get well and eventually develop her limitless potential.

Charles

Charles was a man who appeared shaken, as though he had fought in at least two wars. He had a shell-shocked look about him: hollow and haunted. He had a diagnosis of schizophrenia and moderate mental retardation. Charles had spent a great deal of his life in state psychiatric hospitals. He had actually been both physically and sexually abused by other patients and by staff, by his own account. He would recount story after story of abuse. He even experienced flashbacks. A psychiatrist described him curled in a corner on the floor of her waiting room for over 20 min, refusing to budge, because he was sure that one of the staff members sitting in the waiting room was someone who had physically abused him before and, Charles was convinced, was about to attack him again. No one could calm Charles down.

Charles was actually famous. He was discovered in the state psychiatric hospital by a psychologist who was conducting cognitive evaluations. That psychologist assessed Charles as moderately intellectually disabled and wrote a paper on the phenomenon of misplaced people with developmental disabilities who were populating the long-term inpatient psychiatric units. Following publication of that paper, Charles became well known. He was profiled in books about diagnostics, and the newspapers came to take his picture. Sadly, Charles was aware of the origin of his fame and continued to ask psychologists whenever he encountered one to give him "the test with the blocks" again. "I can pass it this time," he would plead.

Charles was living in an agency that served people with intellectual disability. There, he had a behavior plan because he smoked and he sometimes became upset and destroyed property. The plan placed him on a cigarette schedule of one cigarette every hour, so that he would not smoke all of his cigarettes and then experience extreme frustration when he ran out of them. The plan also addressed preventing property destruction. An involved functional assessment had been conducted, which found that Charles destroyed property to communicate, usually to convey his frustration and humiliation. Charles had a speech impediment as well. He often couldn't communicate the feelings that he had. He would also complain that the staff "treated him like a dog."

One evening Charles was frustrated. A staff person had told him that he needed to go to bed at 10 p.m. "I need another cigarette," Charles stated. Staff said no. However, staff had misinterpreted the plan—there was no curfew on cigarettes. But the staff member was empowered by the restrictive in the plan and felt he was in charge of Charles's cigarettes.

Charles later stated that he felt hurt and humiliated by the way that staff wouldn't let him have his cigarettes and forced him to go to bed at a certain time. When Charles was told to go to bed, he went upstairs for a period of time. He later came back down and told the staff, "I just took a bunch of pills and I'm going to kill myself," then laid down on the couch and went to sleep. The staff tried to move him, but he could not be budged. One hour later, another staff person came into the home for the 11-to-7 shift.

The night-shift fellow, Tom, asked what was wrong with Charles. The other staff person explained: "He won't wake up. Help me get him upstairs, okay?"

"What?" asked Tom.

"He said he had taken pills and flopped on the couch. He was mad 'cause I wouldn't give him another cigarette."

Without listening further, Tom ran upstairs. He found several bubble packs with missing Depakote pills. He ran downstairs and tried to wake up Charles. Charles would not respond. In a panic, Tom called 911. It turns out that Tom's call to 911 came not a moment too soon. Charles was rushed to the hospital, where he remained in a coma for 4 days. He came very close to dying. Doctors estimated that even a few minutes' more delay in the 911 call might have led to Charles's death.

After Charles recovered, the plan was changed. His therapy hours were increased, and the serious trauma work was begun. Charles was allowed to keep his cigarettes, and with all the therapy and improved quality of staff, he stopped destroying property. In an ideal world, he would also have received speech therapy.

Charles actually showed certain physical signs of the genetic disorder Joubert syndrome. He walked with an imbalance, indicating possible akathisia. He had eye problems and speech problems but appeared to be actually quite intelligent, although the insight that he demonstrated did not manifest in the IQ testing done in the hospital. These are signs that may suggest Joubert syndrome (Gitten, Dede, Fennel, Quisling, & Maria, 1998). His facial features also bore a resemblance to those of individuals with Joubert syndrome. This compounds the picture because individuals with Joubert syndrome have acute receptive skills but difficulty with expression. It would follow that, despite a good deal of innate intelligence, they would score poorly on IQ assessments due to their expressive difficulties. Charles fit this pattern and was tortured by having a diagnosis of intellectual disability and being treated differently

Whether or not Charles had Joubert syndrome, he was not well served by the behavior plan, which was so readily misinterpreted by staff. His difficulties were oversimplified as mere behavioral episodes that could be controlled through a manipulation of consequences and contingencies, and as a result, his PTSD went unaddressed. Charles finally felt he had no choice but to kill himself out of hopelessness and frustration. Until he finally received appropriate treatment, these feelings became stronger and stronger. Charles's emotions and trauma, not his aberrant behaviors or his low IQ score, were the real sources of his suffering.

Kali

Kali is a young woman who was born to a crack addict and spent the first 2 years of her life sleeping on the street, eating out of garbage cans, and bouncing from shelter to shelter. She appeared to have been a source of income and nothing more to her mother. She finally was taken by Child Protective Services and placed in foster care.

After several placements, Kali was finally settled in one foster care home. Kali reports that she was told by her foster care family that they had taken her only for the money. Kali also reports that her foster care mother had "anger management issues."

One day, her foster mother actually pushed Kali down the stairs during an altercation. Kali had a broken arm and several bruised ribs. At the emergency room, Kali was told to say she fell unless she wanted to "pay for it" when they got home.

When Kali reached adolescence, hormones kicked in and so did aggression. She quickly lost her foster care placement and found herself in a group home for teenage girls. There she learned the fine art of street fighting and bounced from program to program. She finally exhausted all resources in Maryland and ended up in another. She was placed in an institution and isolated from the other residents.

When talking about her childhood, the statement that brings the strongest emotional response from Kali is "I have never had any friends." Her deeply felt isolation added to her depression, which ignited further aggression, which in turn caused staff to isolate her further.

In the middle of this ongoing cycle, Kali turned 21. On the day of her 21st birthday, Kali was put on a plane and sent back to Maryland. She was greeted by someone whom she had met just once and was hastily placed in a community-based agency for adults with developmental disabilities. The agency struggled to serve her. She was aggressive from time to time, particularly with staff she did not like. She cut herself, she bruised herself, and she attempted to set a fire. If Kali wanted to hurt herself but found that all sharp objects were locked away, she would break a window or a mirror and slice her skin with a piece of glass.

A behavior plan was written and implemented for Kali, and therapy was begun. Rewards were provided through the plan, but time and again, when she was within a day of earning a reward, she would cut herself or attack someone. She also made attempts to go to the hospital, she would call 911 and said she wanted to die or that she was having trouble breathing. At times, this was where she needed to be. Again and again she would be within 24 hr of earning a reward but then would sabotage her own success. She chose the rewards herself: trips, iPods, or the latest game system. And yet she was almost never able to earn them. She made many accusations and tested her own abilities to get staff fired. The staff worked with her as she abused herself and others.

She could not attend to movies or television and was unable to stay focused. The behavior plan was changed repeatedly. She seemed to be implementing her own plan with a mixture of control and self-destruction. She fought with other individuals at her day program. Eventually, after continual staff turnover, Kali was finally left with those who had proved they cared, and she began to stop hurting herself and others. Her rewards were earned more easily, and she began to talk about her feelings rather than demonstrate them. This took over 2 years. She began to see herself as someone others cared about, and she learned ways to express feelings that helped rather than hurt her. The road has been long, however, and she is never certain of continued success.

Applications

In each of these cases, the behavior management plan was not helpful. In some cases, it misdirected the staff; in others, the focus was on behavior, and thus the true diagnosis was missed; in yet others, it was used by staff to create a power differential and fuel a power struggle. In each case, the solution somehow became either the problem or part of it.

Each of these scenarios is a true story. Although their individual stories and backgrounds diverge, Denny, Leslie, Charles, and Kali share a common experience: It was the behavioral manifestations of their problems that were treated rather than the problems themselves, which is tantamount to treating the symptoms without addressing the cause. Below we revisit each case to pinpoint caregivers' missteps and identify what could—and should—have been done differently.

Denny and Restraints

With Denny, the staff were trained to use restraints only as a measure of last possible resort. However, once the restraints were introduced, they were more readily used. And being restrained caused Denny intense fear: He felt retraumatized and was unable to experience any sense of safety in his new environments. Change is very difficult for most people, and this difficulty is only intensified when one perceives a lack of control over many factors in life. People with intellectual disability cannot control who is working with them or how they are being worked with or talked to in most instances. Change, therefore, can be terrifying.

To compound the impact of change, there was the past trauma that Denny had experienced and the fact that he was, in all likelihood, experiencing either a flashback, in which trauma is relived, or a memory of past trauma. This was triggered by the presence of the program manager, a lovely woman with straight blond hair, who may have reminded him of someone who was associated with past abuse or trauma. Every time she came into his physical environment he began throwing tables and chairs. She was very kind to him but that had no effect, clearly someone with staright blond hair had done something to him once, or had been present when something had occurred. Denny's theory that he was unsafe in his new setting was only confirmed when staff restrained him. His only defense was to threaten more aggression, which in turn led to more restraining. This negative cycle was actually perpetuated by the behavior management plan. If Denny had been correctly diagnosed with PTSD, he would have been treated much differently. The focus would have been on keeping him safe. Instead, the underlying condition was missed due to the focus of the psychologist on Denny's behavior.

The symptom was mistakenly seen as the problem. Other, more verbal, individuals with intellectual disability have described the abuse that they endured while resident in the institution where Denny formerly lived. They reported physical and sexual abuse, from both staff and residents. There were times when there were only two staff members to care for 100 residents. One man described a situation in which staff broke his arm and then refused to let him go to the doctor because the abuse would have been exposed. Instead, his arm healed in an odd, crooked shape and remains that way today. Many such stories of abuse have been recounted about life in similar institutions all over the country (Primo & Rivera, 1972). So although Denny did not have the verbal skills to describe what he had been through, it can be assumed that it was extreme. His symptoms of PTSD resulting from this abuse were mistaken for deliberate behaviors that needed to be controlled.

That was many years ago. Today, a functional assessment would have been conducted, and the conclusion might have been that the function of Denny's behavior was to provide escape from the presence of certain people. However, the underlying condition of PTSD is likely to have still been missed if the psychologist viewed Denny's actions as intentional manipulation of his environment in order to escape the presence of certain others. When behavior is the focus, the underlying condition is often missed. The tip of the iceberg does not give any indication of the shape or depth of the iceberg. To continue with the analogy, eliminating the tip might cause someone to miss the iceberg entirely.

Leslie and Noncompliance

In keeping with the idea of the solution being the problem, Leslie's true condition of acute mental illness combined with significant intelligence was entirely missed due to the focus of the behavior management plan on "noncompliance." Leslie learned the actions and mannerisms of someone with a developmental disability because she had been placed in a state institution for individuals with intellectual disability as a child. Mental illness was seen as a disorder that struck in late adolescence or early adulthood in those days; little was known then about childhood onset of mental illness (Carr, 2001).

If Leslie had been born in the 1990s, she would have been diagnosed with childhood schizophrenia or with early-onset schizoaffective disorder. Instead, although her teachers and mental health professionals correctly perceived that there was, in fact, a problem, the prevailing wisdom of the time led them to advise that she be placed, for the rest of her life, in the local institution for the "mentally retarded." Leslie, misplaced, lonely, and struggling with mental illness, adjusted to the best of her ability.

Years later she was viewed as someone who needed to be behaviorally controlled. Thus, it was her behaviors that the professionals focused on, missing entirely her abilities in language and insights into herself and others. Her schizophrenia was also undiagnosed. She was given therapy and was finally understood only after behavior programming had failed to control her actions; she died when appropriate medication lethally interacted with the medication she was already receiving. The irony of this situation is profound. Correctly understood, she could finally be treated, but the medication regime was improperly initiated.

Had Leslie been correctly understood rather than seen only as the sum of her non-compliant behaviors, she would have been on proper medication from the onset. This could have happened in her early adult years if treatment had not been focused on the goal of controlling her aberrant behaviors.

Kali and "the Carrot"

Kali was consistently told and shown, as a child, that she was not worth much to anyone. She internalized this view of herself, as demonstrated through her actions of self-mutilation, her lack of effort toward tasks, and her lack of self-care. Kali told others in a myriad of ways, "I am worth nothing to the people who brought me into this world and, now, to myself."

The critical issue, then, becomes to what extent others can help Kali to build a sense of self-worth and positive identity. The rebuilding required is vast. Kali is like a canyon, with a great gaping hole where there should have been a sense of self. As she tried again and again to demonstrate this lack, others reinforced it by labeling her a "behavior problem," a "difficult child," and later a "difficult-to-place youth-in-transition." Kali heard and reflected all of these labels. She proved others right to the best of her ability. The task at hand, once Kali entered the program for adults with disabilities, should ideally have been to work on building a positive sense of self and, on top of that sense, self-esteem. Instead, the focus of treatment was the behavior plan, and Kali was able to strengthen her own sense of failure by failing again and again to gain the reward or incentive.

The behavior plan was a setup for Kali. She could prove her worthlessness by losing her incentive at the crucial moment and then telling others, "See, this is who I am. I mess everything up." Certain staff fed into this and lectured her on "ruining things" and her "bad attitude" while continuing to implement the plan in a well-intended manner.

Kali did not need that plan. What she really needed was a way to see herself differently. A mirror with a kinder light, so to speak, was required. Eventually, staff and a therapist were able to work on providing such a mirror but only after several years of failed incentives, with Kali conveying to others, "It doesn't matter what you try to give me—I will screw it up because I always screw everything up."

The stress created by the pressure staff felt to get Kali to earn her reward combined with Kali's determination to sabotage the reward took its toll on Kali's relationship with staff. Consequently, the relationship deteriorated, and further power struggles ensued. It wasn't until staff shifted their focus on helping Kali to increase her self-esteem and positive sense of who she was that Kali's relationship with staff improved. When Kali herself and Kali's feeling about herself became the focus, she was able to relax and begin to enjoy her life. Then, in a natural manner, her difficult behaviors decreased radically, and her relationship with those around her improved significantly.

Charles and the Smoking Schedule

Charles did not choose to have his cigarettes restricted. Instead, he was shown a behavior plan and told to sign off on it, while staff were trained to implement it. There were many targeted behaviors, and staff were told what to do in order to reduce negative behaviors. Staff were not told what to do in order to help Charles overcome the effects of the trauma he had endured or how to address his self-destructive, even suicidal, tendencies or to help him to have hope for his future. They were merely taught how to keep his behavior under control. Behaviors, not the person, were the focus.

Unfortunatly, some behavior plans communicate to staff that behaviors, not the human being performing them, are what count. I, myself, have written such plans in the past. We sometimes miss the person in the analysis of the behavior. In many places, staff are taught how to count these behaviors and are evaluated on their ability to count consistently. Staff are not always taught how to help an individual with a disability to have hope for his or her life. They are not always taught how to assist individuals to develop social skills. Often, they are not taught how to help their clients to develop and sustain long-term relationships. Staff are taught mainly how to control individuals' behaviors. Attempts to control another person will frequently set up power struggles. An innocent staff person, trying to implement behavioral control procedures, may inadvertently fall into patterns that create ongoing power struggles that might produce results directly opposite of what is intended. In addition, this very approach might also set up a power differential between staff and individuals that could invite oppression.

Through the plan, the staff were given the message that they were in control of both Charles and his cigarettes. They were tasked with managing Charles's smoking and his behaviors. Charles, however, never bought into the cigarette schedule and never said he wanted to cut down or quit. So he saw staff as the oppressor. Staff did not attend to the details of the cigarette schedule, which allowed Charles to smoke once an hour; instead, they understood the power situation. One member of staff, feeling empowered, told Charles that he could not smoke after 10 p.m.—following the intent but not the actual details of the plan. This frequently occurs when behavior plans are implemented in residential settings with adults. These same tools may be very helpful in teaching new behaviors and breaking bad habits for children, but as individuals with ID mature and seek to find a meaningful life, such procedures may become inadvertently oppressive.

The final power that Charles attempted to regain in the face of this perceived oppression was the power to take his own life. It is quite possible that, in his mind, that was the only power left to him. Those with PTSD often view such an act as their only recourse. The correlation between suicide and PTSD is very high (Herman, 1997). If the staff had had training on PTSD and individuals with ID, perhaps that particular staff member who had interacted with Charles on the night he tried to kill himself would have taken Charles's threats more seriously. Instead, staff were trained on the management of behaviors and could see only Charles's behavior, not Charles himself and the agony of his day-to-day life.

Summary

It is possible that a strictly behavioral approach to the issues of adults with ID restricts treatment and understanding of their true diagnosis and treatment needs. In fact, at times, it may exacerbate symptoms and worsens the condition of the individual. I believe that we are often looking at the effects of trauma and that these effects are actually at the root of many behavioral difficulties.

Wigham, Hatton, and Taylor (2011) published a literature review in which they examined the ways that trauma affects individuals with ID. They concluded that the measures used were not standardized to individuals with ID, and thus the methodologies of such studies were compromised. They asserted that there is a serious need to understand and study the effects of trauma on individuals with ID and that, heretofore, that need has not been met. Since we are faced with a dearth of research in this area, we are forced to examine various case studies in order to examine the possibility that the root of so many behavioral difficulties is actually repeated exposure to trauma and related trauma-based responses.

The cases described in this chapter illustrate some of the ways in which traditional behavioral treatment actually may harm the individual with ID and further traumatize individuals. Actual symptoms of PTSD may be misunderstood as behavioral disorders; symptoms of mental illness may also be misunderstood and approached behaviorally. Genetic disorders, fetal alcohol and fetal cocaine damage, and their associated behavioral patterns are often ignored or misdiagnosed as well. Treating only the behaviors manifested as a result of these diagnoses may cause us to miss the underlying issues with which an individual may be grappling.

References

Carr, A. (2001). *Abnormal psychology.* Sussex, England: Psychology Press.

Gitten, J., Dede, D., Fennel, E., Quisling, R., & Maria, B. (1998). Neurobehavioral development in Joubert syndrome. *Journal of Child Neurology, 13,* 391–397.

Herman, J. (1997). *Trauma and recovery.* New York: Basic Books.

Mahoney, M. J. (2002). Constructivism and positive psychology. In C. R. Snyder & S. J. Lopez (Eds.), *Oxford handbook of positive psychology* (pp. 745–750). Oxford, England: Oxford University Press.

Primo, A. T. (Producer), & Rivera, G. (Correspondent). (1972). *Willowbrook: The last great disgrace* [Video].

Tiihonen, J., Lonngvist, J., Wahlbeck, K., Klaukka, T., Niskanen, L., Tanskanen, A., & Haukka, J. (2009). 11-year follow-up of mortality in patients with schizophrenia: A population-based cohort study (FIN11 study). *Lancet, 374,* 620–627.

Wigham, S., Hatton, C., & Taylor, J. (2011). The effects of traumatizing life events on people with intellectual disabilities: A systematic review. *Journal of Mental Health Research in Intellectual Disabilities, 4,* 19–39.

The Functionality of the Functional Assessment

The functional assessment was derived from the functional analysis, pioneered by Brian Iwata (Clements & Martin, 2002) and others at the Kennedy Kreiger Institute. It is, in essence, a microanalysis of the elements involved in a behavior being performed. What happens before (the antecedents), what happens after, the consequences and their nature, and the schedule according to which these contingencies occur are analyzed in conjunction with the performance of the behavior. The behavior being performed is usually of negative valence or maladaptive. The functional analysis is traditionally conducted in a controlled setting, such as an institution, hospital, or classroom (Catania, 1984).

Functional analysis has been used frequently to address behavioral issues of adults with ID in controlled settings. When these individuals moved to settings that were more community based, a looser approach to analysis from the applied behavioral analysis school was adapted: the functional assessment. The functional assessment works on the same assumptions as the functional analysis. The goal of controlling an individual's behavior is the same: to rid the individual of maladaptive behaviors and replace those maladaptive behaviors with more positive, adaptive behaviors. The fundamental assumption is that both the individual and the environment can be controlled by the skilled worker.

There are several underlying assumptions of this transition from the clinical setting to the community, from functional analysis to functional assessment, that are highly questionable. The first assumption is that environmental contingencies can be controlled in community settings, meaning that antecedents can be determined and consequences can be delivered in a controlled manner. The second assumption is that adults with ID are performing behaviors in order to arrive at a desired consequence and, therefore, deliberately manipulating their environment in order to derive gain. The third assumption is that a change within an individual can be effected by changing the environmental contingencies, or rewards and punishments—in other words, that change in behavior comes and is sustained by changes in the environment, rather than by internal changes in the individual. In this chapter, I explore each of these assumptions.

Community Versus Controlled Settings

Within a controlled setting, the antecedents or events that occur prior to a behavior and the consequences, the events occurring after a behavior, and the schedule of reinforcement and reward can be carefully measured and manipulated. However, in a community setting, these controls are not in place. Anything could be occurring prior to onset of a behavior. Staff could record one antecedent, assuming that it was the trigger event of the behavior of an individual, but an entirely different event, unnoted by staff, could have, in actuality, triggered the behavior.

For example, let's say that Tom becomes aggressive and hits his housemate right after dinner, when it is time to do his chores. After that, Tom is told to leave the area and calm down. Most functional assessments would view this behavior as functioning to provide an escape for Tom from doing his chores. This may be true; however, what if there are other factors at play? Maybe Tom was ridiculed that day at his job and made to do extra work. Maybe Tom's housemate said something to Tom in a teasing manner that reminded him of the ridicule. Maybe Tom's housemate refused to do sexual favors for Tom, which the housemate, until recently, had been doing after dinner in exchange for cigarettes. I have encountered all of these factors, variables arising from beneath the surface. They are usually not detected in a functional analysis and may not ever be known.

Another example might be of an individual who has a severe intellectual disability and is performing self-injurious behaviors (SIB). Let us say that the functional analysis reveals that the antecedents of Bobby's SIB behaviors are often activities in the home, such as the other housemates watching television or playing games, in which Bobby is not included. Bobby will, at those times, begin to hit himself repeatedly on the head or scratch himself. The consequence is that after Bobby does this, the staff come over to him, tell him to stop, and give him attention.

A functional assessment, conducted by a psychologist who comes into the home and gets the picture of the antecedents, behaviors, and consequences and looks at the frequency of the occurrences of the behaviors is likely to conclude that the function of Bobby's SIB behavior is to gain attention. A psychologist who conducts a more detailed functional assessment may also conclude that the activities that are occurring before Bobby engages in SIB are not activities that Bobby enjoys. The psychologist might observe that Bobby does not like or understand the TV shows that the others watch, and he does not like or understand those games that others play. The psychologist conducting the functional assessment might then conclude that the SIB behaviors are also functioning to provide stimulation because Bobby is bored and has no activities available to him that he enjoys.

The functional alternative might be to engage in activities with staff that are enjoyable to Bobby. This behavior would be shaped by rewarding Bobby each time he asked staff to bounce a ball with him. Perhaps the value of this would be that Bobby would gain more time with staff and staff would learn to interact recreationally with Bobby.

However, what if Bobby actually is autistic and is overly stimulated by the noise of the television and the game playing? What if Bobby actually feels anxious and is looking to soothe himself by performing SIB behaviors? Perhaps the SIB behaviors cause endorphins to be released, as some researchers assert (Sandman, Touchette, Lenjavi, Marion, & Chicz-DeMet, 2003). Perhaps Bobby is really in need of a quiet place to decompress after a stimulating day at the day program. Perhaps Bobby was experiencing anxiety as a result of changes in staff. Maybe the psychologist is unaware of the impact that the changes in staff have had on Bobby.

In the community, many, many factors can be easily missed. As illustrated by these two examples, there are more antecedents than can ever be measured. In addition, there are also secondary gains from behavioral episodes that may not be able to be detected or understood.

How can data taken ever reflect the many stimuli that occur in community settings? How can the gains from those behaviors, so complex and, at times, obscure, all be measured? How can we ever know, let alone measure, the effects of daily interactions with van drivers, co-residents, people in the community including neighbors, staff, substitute staff, and managers who may drop in?

In the isolated settings in which the functional analyses are conducted, these interactions are known; often they are with the people taking the actual data or delivering the reinforcers. However, in the community, these interactions are not controlled and may provide stimulation or triggers that have not been recorded.

Take a minute, if you please, and make a list of your six most positive behaviors in the last month and your six most negative behaviors during that same time period. Now look at the list of negative behaviors. Write down beside each negative behavior whether the behavior was

1. An effort to gain a specific consequence, thus providing a way for you to get something you needed, such as attention or escape or communication.
2. A pure, unthinking response to a trigger in your environment, much in the way that Pavlov's dogs salivated when they heard a tone before feeding time.
3. An expression of emotion not designed by you to produce a certain effect. Was it based on feelings that were occurring within you?

What was the result of your self-report? When I have conducted this exercise, most people reported that their negative behaviors were the product of some emotional state rather than deliberately designed to produce a certain response from the environment.

Why should we think that individuals with ID are any different from us? Do we believe that having a slightly lower IQ causes someone to be able to better control their emotions and to deliberately manipulate others through their behaviors? Can they carefully assess what function their behavior will provide, what needs will be deliberately met through their negative behaviors? Maybe a few individuals can and do, but I would argue that people's more extreme actions, or behaviors, express their emotion.

Emotion Versus Manipulation

Behavior is, in itself, a language—but not such a deliberate one as many behaviorists have assumed. In many cases, it is a language of emotion. When language itself is impaired, then actions become language. Even those of us who can speak and talk in detail about our emotion often do not do so. Instead, we allow these emotions to build until they erupt, not always in the most desirable manner. If we can express these feelings verbally, we are usually less likely to express them behaviorally. The same is true for people with ID.

Behaviors based on emotion may be misinterpreted as manipulative. If a functional assessment is conducted, it is actually not unusual, in my experience, that the assessment will miss the emotional component behind the behavioral issue. Here are a few possible examples to illustrate this point.

Marianne

Suppose that Marianne is a young woman with Down syndrome, who goes to the mall with her staff one evening. There Marianne encounters some teenagers who are rude and who loudly use the R word. This is not unimaginable. Let us say that Marianne hears this, and it triggers bad feelings from her days of being in school, where other children teased her, used that word frequently, and told her she would never be able to do anything right. "You can't do it!" they would say.

Let us imagine that Marianne hears the teenagers at the mall and the memory of those children floods her. She becomes upset, but her caring staff are able to calm her down for the time being. They go somewhere for a bite to eat, and Marianne is fine again.

The next day Marianne is at work and is given a new task. It is not complicated. However, Marianne tries to do the new task and does not master it right away. Instead of trying again, as she has in the past, she becomes angry. She hears the children and the teenagers calling her the R word and remembers the children saying that she would never be able to anything right. At that point, Marianne gets up and flips the work table over. She screams and says she's not doing this anymore. Staff comfort her and allow Marianne to sit in the lounge area for the rest of the day. Staff report the incident. It happens again the next day, when the new task is presented. This time, Marianne says that she doesn't want to do it but the staff encourage her to try. On the first try, Marianne does not succeed at the task and again flips the table. This time she curses at everyone around her as well. The staff again comfort her, take her out of the work area, and allow her to remain in the lounge area for most of the day. Again, the staff report the incident.

The psychologist is called in because there have been two serious incidents indicating that there is a behavioral issue. Conducting the functional analysis, the psychologist will most likely look at the consistent trigger, or antecedent, of the table-flipping behavior as the introduction of the new task. The psychologist will then look at the consequence: Marianne is able to go to the lounge area and no longer engage in attempting to complete the task. The psychologist is likely to conclude that the function or purpose of the behavior is to provide an escape from the new task. If the psychologist asks what is going on at home, whatever is reported will not appear as an antecedent because the behavior did not occur at home. "She's fine at home" is what we are often told when we psychologists investigate episodes during the day. Residential staff are likely to have long forgotten the incident at the mall.

In actuality, Marianne is suffering with the low self-esteem that the R-word label provokes in her and with a lack of a positive sense of identity. She sees herself only as someone who can't. The new task and her early, unsuccessful efforts to complete it represent confirmation that she is the person who "cannot do." The person who does not fit in and has been labeled horrible names is the same person who can't do tasks and can't learn new things. In response to the negative emotions provoked by the negative view of herself, Marianne becomes upset. It's true, she might think, "I am a [R word]. I can't do anything right. I am a failure."

Then the psychologist who comes in assesses her as someone who is manipulating her environment through her behavior in order to get out of doing the new task. So rather than instruct the staff to teach her the task more slowly and to verbally build up her sense of herself, a plan is written to address the need for escape and provide choices for Marianne. The psychologist writes a plan in which the staff give Marianne a choice of what to do that day. Marianne chooses old, familiar tasks. Marianne is affirming her low self-esteem and thinking the staff know that she can't do the new task and will never do it correctly, so the staff are giving her a way out because they feel sorry for her. Marianne picks the easier and familiar task with a sense of defeat, an acknowledgment that she is less capable than those around her.

She stops flipping the table, and the psychologist is seen as successful. Marianne gives up ever hoping to learn the new task. If staff had worked through Marianne's fear and self-hatred and supported her in learning the new task, she could have fought against her negative view of herself, armed with the ammunition of accomplishment. Instead, the behavior plan unwittingly reinforces her negative view of herself. Maybe she also now sees herself as a behavior problem because she is one of the individuals in the program who has a behavior plan.

Joanne

Another common situation in which a functional assessment might cause the underlying issue to be missed is when there are emotionally driven attention-seeking behaviors. Let's take Joanne, for example. Joanne is a young woman who was sexually abused by her stepfather from age 4 to 9. After that she was put in foster care and basically neglected. As a teenager, she returned to her mother, now divorced from the stepfather, and was again sexually molested, this time by the mother's boyfriend. Joanne believes that the only time that she has received love in her life has been when she was performing sexual favors. She believes that this is her value to others, in particular to men. She is eager to continue performing favors in order to continue receiving what is her idea of love and validation.

Joanne is highly promiscuous at the day program. She flirts with different men, gives sexual favors in the bathroom, attempts to seduce male staff, and even engages in sexual activity one afternoon under the van with the man she prefers the most. The psychologist is called in, and the functional assessment that is conducted indicates that Joanne is performing these behaviors in order to gain attention. A plan is implemented in which she is not given attention for being sexual, but only for socially appropriate interactions. She is praised for appropriateness; everyone is encouraged to ignore her other overtures.

The plan may work. If the agency is more progressive, they may even support Joanne in picking one of these men to date. Unfortunately, however, Joanne never receives the care she really needs. She does not tell anyone about her history of sexual abuse because it causes her to feel shame when she discusses it. However, if someone had taken the time to talk to Joanne about how she feels inside while performing her promiscuous behaviors, then they might have discovered that she only feels valuable when offering sexual services. She does not feel that she will ever be valued for the other aspects of who she is. Sadly, Joanne is never able to open up and does not get counseling or treatment. Instead, she accepts everyone's reduction of her as an individual with "inappropriate social behaviors." Her sense of identity has shifted from being someone who is worthy only because of her sexual ability to being someone who is scorned for her promiscuity, who is labeled as a behavior problem, and who requires a behavior plan. Her real needs are never met, and the real cause of her behavior is never unearthed.

The Quantification of Emotions

The underlying assumption in these examples of misunderstood behavioral issues is that the root of many, if not most, behavioral issues seen with individuals with ID is essentially emotional in nature. This is an assumption that is difficult to measure. The assumption underlying the functional assessment is that the behavior is providing some kind of gain. It is assumed that the behavior will continue as long as gain continues to be provided, whether through attention or escape. When the gain changes, the behavior changes as well. This assumption appears easy to measure: Measuring the behavior, measuring both the antecedents setting the stage and the gains, and manipulating the gains and the behavior changes all lead to successful behavioral changes.

There are some fundamental flaws with this logic, however. One flaw is that the measuring itself provides attention; changing the gain includes the introduction of a behavior plan, the presence of professionals, and the consent of the individual, which includes extra interaction with that individual on the part of the professionals. The individual may feel now that he or she is being expected to perform well in order to support the reputation of the professional or the job security of the staff. There may be a myriad of motives associated with the individual's desire to change his or her behavior after the introduction of a behavior plan that have nothing to do with the gain being provided.

The individual with a plan receives more overall attention, usually more rewards, and ultimately more encouragement. I have known individuals with ID, in my years of practice, who confided in me that they were upset that only the people who created problems were the ones who were given big rewards. One individual begged me to write a behavior plan for him so he could get more outings like the other individuals who had plans. This person offered to develop some negative behaviors in order to get this plan, and I took great pains to talk him out of it. He was right, however. Having a behavioral issue would have brought him increased attention and rewards for seeming attempts to control that issue. Just having a plan can make life more pleasant when one is stuck in the drab routines of daily life. It is clear that, in many cases, those with behavioral issues get a better level of service. Others see that. Individuals with ID are not stupid.

Is it really valid to count the number of behaviors and then assume that we are looking at behaviors that are under the control of environmental contingencies based on the count we get? How can we assume this when we cannot measure internal stimuli and emotional states? How can we count and quantify expressions of emotion that are expressed in a variety of ways, and any given action can be manifesting a myriad of internal emotional states? These are questions I submit to those wedded to the validity of behavioral data as proof that behaviors of individuals with ID are controlled by environmental contingencies.

Does Correlation Mean Causation?

One further assumption of the functional assessment done in community settings is that when there seems to be a correlation between a behavior and a gain or loss in the environment, or between a series of behaviors and a series of gains or losses, that correlation between behavior and gain or loss means causation. When does correlation equal causation? Any statistician knows that it takes more than a high correlation statistic to prove causation (Bakeman, 1992). How is it that we in the community assume that because we have found correlations between individual's behaviors and what occurs afterward we can assume causation?

For example, Cindy screams whenever it is time for a bath, but when she gets a shower she does not scream. Most of us would conclude that there is something about sitting in a bathtub that causes Cindy discomfort and that she is manipulating her situation in order to get showers, because she prefers them. Suppose we later find out that Cindy was sexually and physically abused as a child while in a bathtub. She is having flashbacks when she sits in the bathtub, although she may actually prefer the warm soaking of the water as opposed to the spray of the shower. We may never know some of these situations. Through the functional assessment we assume that correlations between behaviors and antecedents and consequences equal causation and that by changing the antecedents and consequences we have solved the root of the problem.

Functional assessments in the community often can be misleading. Someone who is in pain may be viewed as manipulative. Someone who has PTSD may be seen as using his or her behavior to escape an obligation or environmental demand due to laziness or a need to control and assert power over staff or the environment. Those who feel badly about themselves may back down on an issue when feeling further devalued and no longer perform a behavior that was, in fact, an expression of emotion and a cry from the depth of their being for validation. Correlation does not mean causation, and functional assessments do not always reveal the actual root cause of the behavior.

FIGURE 1 The Behavioral Pyramid

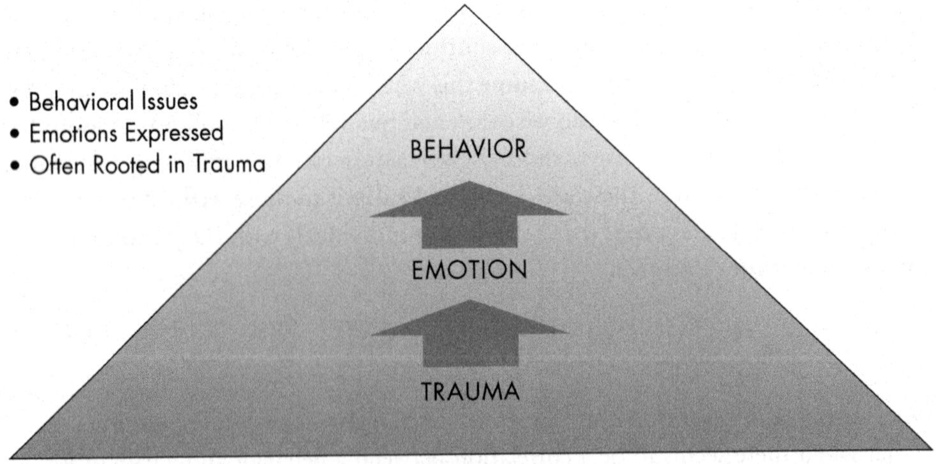

- Behavioral Issues
- Emotions Expressed
- Often Rooted in Trauma

BEHAVIOR

EMOTION

TRAUMA

When we only address the behavior, we miss the true cause and root of difficulties.

As stated earlier, behind the behavior there is often an emotion. Frequently, behind the emotion is an accumulation of past traumas and their effects. For the purposes of understanding individuals with ID, it might be best to view PTSD as a continuum rather than a discrete condition. When people are easily triggered and the trigger cannot be traced to a rational response, it can be viewed as a trauma response and indicate a degree of trauma present (Siegel, 2010). When trauma is still present, the person relieves it, even to a small degree and a response, and although the resulting emotional output can look like a manipulative behavior, it may, in fact, be based on that emotion that stems from the reliving of trauma. Not only is trauma relived, it becomes a present experience: The past becomes the present as the pain is reexperienced. The model of behavior I propose is therefore based on a pyramid structure (see Figure 1), which reflects the source of the behavioral issue. Rather than being a purely manipulative act, the behavior is a reflection of underlying emotion, which is based on even more deeply embedded traumatic experiences.

The Masking of Behavioral Phenotypes and Genetic Disorders

Another difficulty involved in the functional assessment is that it labels what may be characteristics of the individual, possibly genetically based, as deliberate and manipulative behaviors. Certain individuals may have genetic predispositions, or in more extreme examples what are called *behavioral phenotypes*. A behavioral phenotype is a behavioral manifestation of a genetic condition that produces, within the individual, a certain pattern of behavior. That pattern will be individually adapted to people and reflect their own unique characteristics, but there will be common themes and trends among people with certain genetic disorders.

For example, individuals with fragile X are known to have the behavioral phenotype that involves socially withdrawn behaviors as well as behaviors that manifest anxiety, even fight-or-flight trends when social stimulation is increased (Smith, Barker, Seltzer, Abbeduto, & Greenberg, 2012). If an individual who becomes aggressive when there is a social event is taken out of the event to a quiet place that he enjoys, then the functional assessment might indicate that the behavior was performed for the sake of escape. However, the behavior may, in fact, have been a manifestation of fear and anxiety due to the increased social stimulation. If this is the case, and anxiety has overwhelmed the individual with fragile X, then an antianxiety medication along with some self-soothing techniques are best.

Conversely, in a functional assessment, the behavior might be seen as performing the function of escape and the individual would be given choices and rewarded for either making a choice or enduring an uncomfortable situation. The anxiety, which is biologically related and genetically based, will never be appropriately addressed. The functional assessment may oversimplify and actually mask the genetic and biological roots of a behavior. Behavioral phenotypes and, in many cases, the actual genetic disorder may be entirely missed.

Masking of Fetal Alcohol Damage

In *The Broken Cord*, Michael Dorris (1989) told the poignant tale of his adopted son, who has fetal alcohol syndrome (FAS). By reviewing the research as well as recounting his experiences as a parent, Dorris made an eloquent point that individuals with FAS have a very difficult time connecting cause and effect. The sequential reasoning aspects of their brain are broken, so to speak. These individuals can gain many cognitive skills, but they cannot perceive or understand the link between actions and reactions or causes and their effects. For example, an individual with FAS might do something that directly annoys another person and that person may scold the individual with FAS, but the individual will not understand why the annoyed person has scolded him or her. Then the individual may again do the same thing to the person who got annoyed before. The annoyed person will be even more annoyed, scold again, and the individual with FAS might still continue not to comprehend at all why the person is more annoyed and now yelling.

I have had this experience with many individuals with FAS. One in particular, whom we will call Ellen, comes to mind. Ellen had a very loving and concerned family, comprised of brothers and sisters and their children. Ellen's mother had died several years before of breast cancer, and Ellen had lived with her father until he, too, passed away. Ellen had, in fact, helped to take care of her father while he was ailing.

Ellen had moved into a group home with eight residents after her father passed away. I was asked to write a behavior plan for Ellen because each evening she would insult the two most volatile residents and start conflict after conflict. Sometimes the conflicts that she started did not actually involve her, but more often than not, she would be in a yelling match with one or the other of the two volatile residents.

The other residents of the home understood the importance of not agitating the two excitable residents. They would encourage Ellen to stop, but Ellen never stopped. We set up a plan in which Ellen was rewarded with a shopping trip for not agitating others, but week after week, she was unable to earn the trip. We tried encouraging her to earn daily diet sodas; Ellen earned two out of a possible seven. More often than not she would agitate the wrong people. We tried giving Ellen extra attention, assuming, through the functional assessment, that she was agitating others to bring attention to herself. We lavished attention on her and did many special activities with her. Ellen continued to agitate. We set up opportunities for peer attention, deciding that Ellen was interested in that possibly more than the consequence of gaining staff attention. She spent more time with peers of her choice, but still she continued to agitate. We changed the rewards of the plan, offering money for no insulting or teasing. Still there was no result.

One day I was talking with a fellow who attended another program at the agency. He was very bright but struggled with mental illness to the extent that he was unable to focus on anything for long, including IQ tests, and thus he had been labeled as mildly mentally retarded despite his innate intelligence. He told me that there was a lady on his van that looked like she had that "alcohol thing."

"What alcohol thing?" I asked. "You know," he said, "her mother drank when she was still in her stomach." I stared at this very intelligent young man. He had recently told me with an accusing look that "evil psychologists" who gave him "evil IQ tests" had ruined his life. I listened to what he was saying, and then I described Ellen, short with dark straight hair. "Yup" he said, that was whom he meant. It was a great insight. I had never realized that she did, indeed, have the features of fetal alcohol syndrome. I had heard so much from her about how wonderful her mother and brothers and sister were that I couldn't even see what was in front of my face. I met with Ellen and asked her whether her mother had ever consumed alcohol. "She loved her beer!" Ellen exclaimed. "She drank it all the time!"

I realized that Ellen had fetal alcohol syndrome. No matter what we did to present consequences, change reinforcers, or manipulate contingencies, Ellen did not understand the cause-and-effect link between her actions and the effects that they produced. She never understood why people were mad at her and how her actions affected them or produced negative results in the environment.

I was able to talk to the residential director of the agency about moving Ellen. They soon moved her into a three-resident unit with two very calm women. Ellen got along famously with them, they did not pay any attention to Ellen's negative remarks, and all three went happily along with whatever plans the staff presented to them. Ellen was able to live harmoniously with them, they accepted Ellen despite her occasional outbursts, and Ellen was able to get along well with them. I learned to search for the correct diagnosis first before conducting a functional assessment and implementing a behavior plan. The young man from the other day program was one of the best consultants ever.

Summary

I have been involved, in one capacity or another, with each situation described in this chapter or with situations that were very similar. It is important to reflect on the ways in which a functional assessment might mask an underlying situation, might cause a diagnosis to be missed or misunderstood, or might marginalize a critical emotional issue. As a psychologist in the field of intellectual disability, I have long been concerned that functional assessments minimize important emotional and social issues that affect the individual with the intellectual disability. I am specifically addressing adults and their adult needs. For children, these interventions are helpful in teaching the child cause and effect and self-regulation (Catania, 1984). For adults, however, I find the assessments to be reductive at best, oversimplifying complex motives and needs and camouflaging important emotions.

Individuals who have lived the length of time that qualifies them to be an adult should be regarded and respected as adults. Reducing these individuals to bargaining "capitalists" who are always angling for a desired consequence and can be controlled through the manipulation of a consequence is both inaccurate and fundamentally demeaning. A more holistic approach to behavioral change is urgently needed. Moreover, such an approach should be embraced by regulators, executive directors, and clinicians. No one can be an expert in manipulating another person. That will only last for so long. Let us all become experts in fostering growth and positive development. Let us become experts in respect and support.

References

Bakeman, R. (1992). *Understanding social science statistics: A spreadsheet approach.* Hillsdale, NJ: Erlbaum.

Catania, A. C. (1984). *Learning.* Englewood Cliffs, NJ: Prentice Hall.

Clements, J., & Martin, N. (2002). *Assessing behaviors regarded as problematic for people with developmental disabilities.* New York: Jessica Kingsley Publishers.

Dorris, M. (1989). *The broken cord.* New York: Harper & Row.

Sandman, C. A., Touchette, P., Lenjavi, M., Marion, S., & Chicz-DeMet, A. (2003). Beta-endorphin and ACTH are dissociated after self-injury in adults with developmental disabilities. *American Journal of Mental Retardation, 6,* 414–424.

Siegel, D. J. (2010). *The mindful therapist: A clinician's guide to mindsight and neural integration.* New York: W. W. Norton.

Smith, L. E., Barker, E. T., Seltzer, M. M., Abbeduto, L., & Greenberg, J. S. (2012). Behavioral phenotypes of fragile X syndrome in adolescence and adulthood. *American Journal of Intellectual and Developmental Disabilities, 117,* 1–17.

3   Prevention before Intervention

Because applied behavioral therapists largely agree that the four main functions of behavior are attention, escape, stimulation, and communication, it only makes sense that we focus on these arenas proactively rather than reactively (Carr et al., 2006). In other words, if John is having a behavioral issue so that he can receive attention, why don't we give him attention first so that he doesn't have to perform a behavior to get it? If Linda is performing a behavior so that she can escape from a task, why don't we give Linda a choice about what tasks to perform and when to perform them? Then she won't need to get her needs met through her behaviors. If Nancy is putting holes in the wall when she is frustrated and she is nonverbal, let's teach her to use Board Maker (Mayer Johnson, Pittsburgh, PA) and give her a wallet of picture symbols so that she can communicate in other ways. Another useful yet affordable device for communication is the iPad, with a variety of applications available to enhance communication. In addition, on an iPad actual pictures of the targeted object of communication can be used to substitute for the picture symbols, which may possibly be misunderstood. If Allen is so bored that he scratches himself to feel sensations, let's teach him to use a vibrator on his skin or to rub lotion on himself before he gets to the point that he has to scratch in order to feel something. Let's have music playing that he enjoys rather than a movie or TV show that he doesn't understand. Let's entertain him and teach him to entertain himself in as many ways as we can come up with so that he doesn't have to hurt himself to experience life.

This may seem like an overly simplistic approach but think *prevention*. If behaviors have four main functions and individuals perform those behaviors to meet a function, then let's just enable them to access what they want without having to perform a negative or positive behavior to get it. Let's anticipate that they are human and they will need attention, choice (a function of escape), ways to communicate, and stimulation.

Imagine if you had to create a ruckus just to get some entertainment in your life. Imagine if the only entertainment was watching a TV show that you didn't understand or going to an activity that you couldn't participate in. If we look at each person with an intellectual disability whom we are serving and assess how we can help them to meet their human needs for choice, attention, entertainment, and communication, we can vastly reduce behavioral incidents and save a significant amount of money on consulting psychologists.

The prevention approach does not require a clinician. On the Web site for the National Association for the Dually Diagnosed (NADD) I have made available a tool I designed (Harvey, 2009) to assess how each individual is being empowered to meet his or her needs. This is not the only way to assess needs and need fulfillment. There are many tools that can be used in a proactive manner to help the individual meet basic human needs without having to behaviorally beg.

Behavior as Performance Art

Of course, there are those who see behavior as a form of performance art. Among the population of individuals with ID, there are those who have certain gifts. Creative gifts may often be present and have little or nothing to do with cognitive skills. I have worked with many individuals who would have enjoyed engaging in theater due to their love of acting and their acting skills. However, they were not afforded such opportunities in their upbringing. Because of this lack of opportunity and frustrated creativity, they chose to use their theatrical gifts for behavioral performance. These performances may be privately scripted or, more often, improvisational.

Rachel, for example, has a gift in the performing arts. She became angry with staff who were going off shift and leaving her rather than staying the night, so she threw all of her valuable belongings, such as her computer, keyboard, and television, out the window so that the departing staff would witness the various crashes. Ann loved to fake seizures. When a gathering of people occurred in her home, she would crash to the floor and shake with one eye open, gauging her effect on her audience.

These acts may be misinterpreted as desperate attempts for attention if the gifts of the actors are overlooked. When more carefully examined, we can see that these are talents just needing to be expressed. Attention is often already abundant for these individuals; what is craved is *audience*. When the audience arrives, the performance begins; or when the dramatic opportunity presents itself, the actor may spontaneously take advantage of the improvisational moment. The element of creativity cannot be overlooked.

Ideally, this creativity can be redirected, but it must never be overlooked when an artist is at work. Gardner (1993) has long asserted that there are many types of intelligence and that only a few of them are measured by IQ testing. Individuals who score below 72 on an IQ test may very well have a variety of other types of intelligence that manifest in creativity, emotional awareness, insight into self, or spatial abilities. In all, he has concluded that there are seven types of intelligences that have been uncovered through his research, which included individuals with developmental disabilities. He asserts that although cognitive deficits may be present, there is still great potential for a variety of other intelligences to exist within the individual.

Baer (1993) compared various theories and correlated research concerning creativity. He concluded that the research does not show that creativity can be trained and that there is much evidence to suggest that it involves a different type of thinking, what has been termed *divergent thinking*, which is not necessarily always correlated with traditional intelligence.

Thus, we may conclude that there are individuals with ID who have a variety of creative ways of thinking and creative abilities but who, because of their limited circumstances, have very few outlets for that creativity. Behavior itself, I assert, has become a creative outlet and undeclared art form for some individuals with ID. Thus, a prevention approach must include the provision of creative outlets so that behavioral creativity is not the art form of choice.

Happiness

Positive psychologists have flipped the script on mental health issues by focusing on how human beings can become happy rather than on how negative emotional conditions exist and thrive. Martin Seligman, seen by many as the father of positive psychology, described the evolution of psychological thinking from B. F. Skinner and behaviorism to a more cognitive and then a more positive approach to changes in behavior. After describing animal studies that he and other psychologists had conducted, he wrote:

> Our findings, along with those thinkers like Noam Chomsky, Jean Piaget, and the information-processing psychologists, served to expand the field of inquiry to the mind and to drive the behaviorists into full retreat. By 1975 the scientific study of mental processes in people and animals displaced the behavior of rats as the favorite subject of doctoral dissertations. (Seligman, 2006, p. 28)

The field of psychology as it applies to adult humans has moved away from behaviorism and the views and approach of B. F. Skinner in every arena except in adults with ID. Somehow, they continue to be regarded and treated by professionals as though advances in the last 30 years had never occurred.

Happiness and Positive Psychology

Martin Seligman helped to initiate the positive psychology movement, which promotes psychological wellness. Seligman has more recently focused on the universal factors involved in achieving happiness, or the construct he now prefers, "well-being" (Seligman, 2006). His research and latest book, *Flourish* (Seligman, 2011), break down the five elements of well-being.

The first element is positive emotion, which is basically pleasure. This is the state in which life is enjoyed in a predominantly passive state. This might include eating a good meal or watching an enjoyable movie. The second element of well-being is engagement. During engagement, people are fully interacting with something in their environment. They may be working on a hobby, playing a game, writing, drawing, or engaging in a creative act. Engaging in the world and enjoying that engagement have been proven to enhance happiness.

In his previous book, *Authentic Happiness,* Seligman (2006) included only three main elements in his construct of happiness: pleasure, engagement, and meaning. In *Flourish,* Seligman (2011) embraced the construct of well-being and added relationships to his list of elements, arguing that relationships are an important aspect of overall well-being. This is true for all humans, he asserted, and there is an enormous body of literature to prove it (Seligman, 2011). Conversely, Seligman asserted that loneliness is at the root of much depression. This is certainly true for individuals with ID. Loneliness can be suffocating, particularly for individuals who already feel alienated from the social world.

The next element of well-being that Seligman added in his recent work is achievement. He asserted that the sense of accomplishment is a critical factor of well-being. He pointed out that many people achieve for the sake of the sense of achievement, which is a positive emotional experience.

Finally, the most rewarding and fulfilling element of happiness is the longest lasting as well. It is the level of meaning. Seligman's research shows that people who have found a sense of purpose in their life and feel that their lives have meaning have the highest level of happiness, even if their level of pleasure or engagement is not high. Having a mission brings a deeper joy to our existence, as spiritual leaders have long taught us.

These principles apply easily to individuals with ID. Those who have found a sense of purpose and meaning are able to live more fulfilling lives than those who are spending their days aimlessly. Take, for example, those individuals with ID who have jobs in which they feel that they are truly needed. I have seen a number of individuals who had behavioral problems, sometimes severe behavioral problems, change their behavior naturally when they find work in which they are needed. Their sense of purpose pervades every level of their existence, and they no longer have a need to defy or disrupt. They are needed.

The same is often seen when two people with ID marry. All of a sudden, someone has a mission as a wife or husband. They find a reason to try hard at work so that they can bring more money home, they try harder with chores at home, their hygiene improves, and so on. This is because they have found a role that gives their life significant meaning and purpose. In addition, they are experiencing the sense of well-being gained through interpersonal relationships, as described by Seligman (2011).

Behavior change can be easily facilitated through finding happiness. It is more quickly and effectively changed through finding happiness: through a sense of purpose and meaning. Examples are endless. In our own lives, the most effective source of behavior change is when we decided to step up to a certain role in life and thus adjust our behavior: from student to professional, from player and dater to spouse, from young adult to parent—the list grows of the roles many of us have taken on that give our life great meaning and cause us naturally to change our behavior. No external incentives are needed for change to occur in these scenarios. Our own sense of purpose becomes sufficient motivation for far-reaching behavioral change.

The Happiness Assessment and Procedure

Every individual's happiness is different and unique. What gives my life meaning may be unfulfilling to another. What hobbies I enjoy may be boring to someone else. At the Arc Baltimore, an agency that serves people with ID in community settings, we added an assessment of what makes the individual happy to each behavior plan. So, after the required functional assessment is completed, the happiness assessment is then completed. The happiness assessment (Harvey, 2009) assists individuals, by interviewing them and the staff together, in identifying their sources of happiness on the levels of pleasure, engagement, and meaning.

At the Arc Baltimore, we have found that implementing a "happiness procedure" along with the required positive behavioral procedures increases the level of the individual's happiness and drastically reduces behavioral difficulties. Again, people who are happy rarely hurt themselves or others, destroy property, or instigate altercations. They are too busy being happy.

This procedure has been highly effective. In addition, individuals are leading vastly more rewarding and fulfilling lives when the behavior plan requires that procedures to increase happiness on each level are implemented. It may also help individuals reduce the cocktails of psychotropic medications that they may find themselves taking.

Lisa, for example, found meaning in her role as girlfriend when the staff were required through the behavior plan to help facilitate her relationship with Darren. Darren also vastly changed his behavior. Lisa had a history of running away and remaining missing for days on end. Lisa stopped this behavior, however, and found hanging around a lot more appealing when it involved going on dates with Darren. Lisa and Darren are now planning to move in together, and Lisa has not run away once since the couple started dating over a year ago.

It is much simpler to seek to facilitate individuals with ID in finding their happiness than it is to attempt to control the actions of those individuals and reward every correct behavior. They are no longer children. When given entrance into the adult world, they are also given hope and access to a much more extensive and rich adult life. This is a life that presents inclusion into the world from which they have otherwise been excluded. They no longer have to perform behavioral acts to express anger and despair. Instead, they are busy pursuing an engaged and meaningful adult life. There is little time left, when someone is busy and happy, for creating problems.

Summary

Most individuals who are unhappy and communicating unhappiness through actions undergo significant changes when the chance to pursue happiness arises. Most individuals who are bored and creating problems as a result of boredom do not have behavioral difficulties when they are involved in pursuing their happiness. Furthermore, most individuals with creative abilities are much happier when their creativity is channeled into areas of engagement and meaning rather than behavioral performance art. If the needs of the individuals are met and they are allowed to pursue their happiness, they no longer have to use their behavior to procure the fulfillment of their needs. Their actions can be focused on enhancing their pleasure, engagement, and meaning, and staff can be happiness coaches rather than behavioral controllers.

References

Baer, J. (1993). *Creativity and divergent thinking: A task specific approach.* Hillsdale, NJ: Erlbaum.

Carr, E., Levin, L., McConnachie, G., Carlson, J., Kemp, D., & Smith, C. (2006). *Communication-based intervention for problem behavior: A user's guide for producing positive change.* Baltimore, MD: Paul H. Brookes.

Gardner, H. (1993). *Multiple intelligences: The theory in practice.* New York: Basic.

Harvey, K. (2009). *Happiness assessment.* Available at http://pid.thenadd.org/Happiness%20 Assessment.pdf

Seligman, M. (2006). *Authentic happiness.* New York: Vintage Books.

Seligman, M. (2011). *Flourish.* New York: Free Press.

4

The Dangers of Misdiagnosis

Happiness doesn't always come easily. Some individuals have psychiatric issues that produce impairments to fulfillment. Other individuals may have genetic conditions that prove difficult to live with, and others may have damage from alcohol or substances or both. Yet others may have endured trauma that has created a multitude of difficulties that interfere significantly with the pursuit of happiness.

We cannot help people if we do not identify or understand their correct diagnoses. Earlier, there were clear examples of individuals whose diagnoses were missed due to an overemphasis on behavioral manifestations. In many cases, the true diagnosis is missed because it is fundamentally misunderstood. From this point forward, I will focus on the genetic, fetal, and trauma-based origins of behavioral difficulties and how, when these origins are understood and the correct diagnosis is given, individuals with ID can more freely pursue a happier existence.

Genetic Disorders and Behavioral Phenotypes

There are a number of recently identified genetic disorders that are not well known and often go unidentified (Fletcher, Loschen, Stavrakaki, & First, 2008). As stated earlier, the psychiatric and behavioral profiles that are associated with these disorders, commonly referred to as *behavioral phenotypes,* are sometimes misdiagnosed as symptoms of a purely behavioral disorder. This is something that I have been guilty of in the past. In fact, I have a variety of examples of individuals whom I had misunderstood and misdiagnosed until later learning about genetic disorders and linking the individual with the facial features and behavioral phenotype. I would like to share these examples and discuss some of the more misunderstood disorders in an attempt to illustrate the insufficiency of a purely behavioral approach to treatment.

Joubert Syndrome

Debbie was a young woman who used a wheelchair. The muscles in her legs were extremely flaccid, possibly due to hypotonia, and she could not sufficiently use them to walk. She also had difficulties with her eyesight. She would peer at someone from the corner of her eyes, turning her head to the side, to get a better view. When I first met her, she had been referred for counseling by a very frustrated program director. I was told, "We have a behavior plan, but we cannot manage her behavior. We don't know what else to do." As was always the case in the early 1990s, counseling was a last resort. The counseling, in fact, was a final effort to help control her behavior.

Debbie would get upset and urinate on herself rather than ask to be toileted. Her staff members insisted that she knew how to control herself because she would ask to be toileted sometimes. These staff were convinced that she was doing this deliberately. She also complained and cried a great deal. I found out later that she wanted a boyfriend but could not date due to the lack of an available wheelchair van. She wanted to see her family, but they did not come to visit her. She wanted to switch jobs but was told she could not. She wanted staff to listen to her, but the staff person was busy raising her own child in the agency home. She wanted to be friends with her housemates, but they did not like her and made that clear to her.

Many behavior plans were written for Debbie to control her maladaptive behavior of urinating on herself when she was in an emotional situation. The functional analysis in the last plan completed indicated that the function of Debbie's "inappropriate urination" was "attention." She was doing this for attention, and she got that attention by virtue of the fact that staff had to assist in cleaning up the urine as well as washing and changing Debbie's clothes. The plan writer said that staff should give minimal attention to her and not speak with her while assisting her. Debbie got worse instead of better.

By the time I met with her, it was apparent that she felt very hurt and rejected by staff. The more upset Debbie was over issue after issue, the more she urinated. The more she urinated, the angrier staff got with her. Because the professionals had told the staff that Debbie was doing this purposefully in order to gain attention, staff became angrier and angrier with Debbie. Staff followed the behavior plan's instructions to ignore Debbie and keep interaction to a minimum when cleaning Debbie, but staff also generalized her response and ignored Debbie more and more. Other staff followed suit, and pretty soon Debbie was living in a hostile atmosphere of scorn.

I began counseling with Debbie and weeded my way through many layers of isolation, alienation, and abandonment. Debbie was suffering the loss of family attention and staff concern. She was physically dependent on people she knew did not like her. She was scared, angry, and hurt.

Years later I was privileged to attend a conference held by dedicated family members on Joubert syndrome. Their children had Joubert's, and all had various degrees of related difficulties. Several of them physically resembled Debbie. My eyes were opened. As I read the literature, I found that symptoms included not only hypotonia but also problems with the kidney, difficulties with eyesight and ataxia, and the inability to coordinate voluntary muscle movements. A renowned genetic researcher on the subject, Malissa Parisi, told me that the disorder had only very recently been identified and was therefore underdiagnosed (Parisi, 2009).

It occurred to me that Debbie in all likelihood had Joubert syndrome. More than likely she also could not control her bladder muscles, due to the hypotonia and worsened by the ataxia. When she became emotionally distraught, she was probably unable to control her bladder in the way that she could when she was calm. Perhaps conflicts with staff and neglect from her family had caused her original emotional distress, and then the ignoring that was part of the behavior management plan increased her distress and created a negative cycle in which she was unable to control her bladder. She was not urinating deliberately but, rather, was unable to control her bladder muscles due to her physical condition and her emotional distress.

I worked with Debbie for several years. Most important to her was our relationship. I came every week, no matter what. What we talked about, the self-esteem we built, and the issues we processed were all secondary to my weekly appearance. Debbie needed to know that my affection and concern for her were consistent and unconditional. She never urinated on herself when I was around or for the rest of the afternoon and evening. She tried so hard to speak clearly and share everything. She even made jokes to entertain me.

Debbie had several good years after our work together, with new, more caring staff. She passed away as a result of kidney disease. This is actually a common cause of death in individuals with Joubert syndrome. Many individuals with Joubert's receive dialysis and ultimately receive kidney transplants to prolong their lives. Perhaps if we had known that Debbie had Joubert syndrome, she could have received treatment for kidney disease before it was in the latter stages and she might have lived longer. Without a behavior management plan that labeled her urinary incontinence as deliberate attention-seeking behavior, she definitely could have been spared humiliation and emotional distress.

Smith-Magenis Syndrome

A young woman, Shelly, recently came to an agency where I worked. She had been discharged from several other agencies due to her difficult behaviors. She had several problematic behaviors in her repertoire, but clearly the most vexing was that she had a tendency to place objects in her vaginal area. She often had to be taken to the emergency room for assistance in removal of objects, including small hairbrushes, paper clips, toothbrushes, markers, crayons, pen tops, and pushpins. She was frequently obsessed with inserting such objects into her vaginal region. She would repeatedly discuss doing it and eventually find a way, usually sneaking something into the ladies' room at her day program or in the bathroom at home.

Shelly claimed to have been sexually abused, though her mother had stated that it was Shelly's sister, not Shelly, who had experienced abuse. Regardless, Shelly's psychology associate and I assumed that there had been some sort of sexual trauma in Shelly's background and that she was in need of heightened sexual stimulation. In our experience, this was often the case with those individuals who had histories of childhood sexual abuse.

We provided Shelly with sexual devices and encouraged her to masturbate privately. Despite all of these efforts, and her newfound love of masturbation, Shelly continued to insert objects into her vaginal region. One day the psychology staff and I were discussing various genetic disorders, and I realized that Shelly had the exact facial features of someone with Smith-Magenis disorder. It was a startling realization.

The behavioral phenotype, or genetically determined behavioral tendencies, of people with the Smith-Magenis genetic syndrome includes both self-injurious behaviors and, more specifically, "stuffing objects into body orifices" (Allanson, Greenberg, & Smith, 1999). As we reviewed the various Web sites and information on Smith-Magenis, we realized that we had been looking at the tendency that Shelly had to stuff objects into her vagina as a behavioral manifestation of hypersexuality. We had assumed that it was a deliberate behavior with the function of stimulating Shelly sexually in a way that she had learned to be stimulated from childhood trauma. We had also been doing therapy and found it interesting that Shelly had not wanted to do the trauma work we assumed would be needed, instead focusing on current situations with staff and with her mother. Shelly's obsession with stuffing objects into her lower regions fit perfectly with the description of the behavioral tendencies of individuals with Smith-Magenis syndrome.

Angelman Syndrome

Throughout the years of working as a psychologist with individuals with intellectual disability, I have been asked to write plans targeting many unusual behavioral problems. After about 5 years, I began to refuse to write plans addressing certain target behaviors. I would not write a plan for noncompliance. We are all noncompliant in different ways, and I would not write guidelines that would force a free adult to be compliant. Another topic I began to refuse to address was wandering. I was consulting in a day program where the staff asked for plans for wandering. After I observed the people whom they were working with, I realized that the expectation was that these individuals would stay in one seat all day. I myself am incapable of this. I must get up and move around, even while at my own desk, every 30 to 40 min. This is my nature. I could not write a plan that would not allow someone to stretch when needed. The individuals at the program were often doing either nothing or completing the exact same learning task that they had done every other day for a number of years. I began to draw the line.

At that same day program, I was asked to write a program targeting "inappropriate laughing." This was a new one. This adorable young woman was "driving her staff crazy," according to the manager of the program, by laughing incessantly. I was supposed to write a plan to address this. After a week of observation, I found that whenever there was any difficulty or discomfort, Mary would laugh and laugh. The staff felt mocked. After writing a plan I was ashamed of, for inappropriate laughing, I went to the library, where I found a reference for Angelman syndrome. Mary fit the description of someone with the disorder. She had the same wide face, small, wide-set eyes, and giant smile. She did not speak, as so many with this syndrome do not, but she appeared to understand everything. I realized that, in all likelihood, Mary had Angelman syndrome. She was apt to spend a lot of time laughing, as abundant laughter is part of the behavioral phenotype for individuals with Angelman syndrome (Williams, 2010).

Later I met a parent who wanted an evaluation for a teenage son who laughed all the time and did not speak. His stepparent perceived him as defiant and disrespectful due to the laughing and lack of cooperation. This time I was able to quickly perceive the facial features of Angelman syndrome. I was then able to reassure his parents that the boy was expressing his nature rather than being purposefully disrespectful or rude. I was so happy to be able to provide such reassurance, rather than another intervention to reduce laughing.

Fragile X

I was used to working with people with fragile X syndrome who were male. The genetic disorder is manifested in the broken tail of the X chromosome. Males, of course, have only one X chromosome, so if there is a genetic defect, or mutation, with that chromosome, there is a high likelihood of a manifestation of that defect. In females, because they have two X chromosomes, there is more likelihood that the mutation of one chromosome will be masked by the other. This, at least, was the assumption I had made. I had not studied the fragile X literature well enough to realize that the syndrome also occurs in females, though significantly less frequently.

Candy had a very structured behavior plan addressing verbal and physical aggression against others. When I began working with her, she enjoyed cursing at me on one out of every three or four visits. The plan instructed staff to walk away and ignore her when she became verbally aggressive. Staff were supposed to firmly set limits when she was physically aggressive, reprimand her sternly, and then withdraw all attention. The plan, on which I had signed off, interpreted the verbal and physical aggression as functioning to gain attention, which was assumed to be Candy's motivation.

I brought my son to work on Take Your Child to Work Day. Candy became very upset and I took notice. I began to think. On the days that she had become upset with me, there were usually strangers at the work site. Either that or we had gone somewhere together in public. Now she was upset with my son. She asked me why "that kid" was there, and when I explained to her the occasion, she replied that it was "Fire Your Psychologist Day."

On another occasion, I insisted that Candy attend the banquet our agency held each year for the individuals we serve. She sat at the table with my husband, became upset at the crowds, and ended up slapping my husband, who does not work in the field and was taken by surprise. As was I. My colleague suggested that Candy was jealous, but the explanation did not suffice, as Candy had also slapped a few other unrelated people. No one could follow the plan and ignore this. Instead, we assisted her in leaving. She calmed down as soon as she left. She complained about having to go to the banquet at all.

A few weeks later, I was working with a friend on her presentation on individuals with fragile X. We looked on the Web (http://www.fragilex.org/) and saw a picture of a young woman who was the spitting image of Candy, only about 30 years younger. I was shocked. It all made sense. That explained all of Candy's verbal and physical aggression. It wasn't deliberate and hostile. It was an expression, albeit a rude one, of her anxiety. Social anxiety is a dominant characteristic of individuals with fragile X syndrome, particularly when exposed to new people or when in crowded situations (Fraxa, 2010). Candy had been exposed to new people every time that she had exhibited verbal or physical aggression. Her anxiety had been high, and she had lashed out. This is a type of response that my colleagues and I had come to expect from males with fragile X syndrome. We made a point of assisting our individuals with fragile X to feel safe and to avoid crowded or socially uncomfortable situations. However, I had never made the connection with Candy. Instead, I had condoned a plan that enforced the withdrawal of social attention from those with whom Candy actually felt comfortable at the times when she most needed their support and sensitivity. When she felt that social anxiety, we could have supported her, assisted her in removing herself from the individuals who were unknown to her or from the crowds, and helped her to calm herself. Instead we continued on until she had an outburst of anxiety, and then we withdrew attention. Because of the plan, we missed the opportunity to assist her in the management of her anxiety and to teach her to self-soothe and remove herself from difficult situations.

Ironically, the presentation that my colleague was working on presented exactly such a protocol. She had been very successful in helping a man with fragile X to manage his social anxiety, even going to McDonald's with him regularly during the lunch rush so that he could learn to reduce his own anxiety around crowds. Her in-the-moment emotional support of him had assisted him in working through his anxiety in the situation. If I had correctly diagnosed Candy's genetic condition, maybe we would have understood how to help Candy manage her anxiety rather than treating her in a way that only exacerbated it.

Summary

As the reader has probably surmised, I have learned the most from my worst mistakes. I have learned, again and again, to look deeper—to look beyond the immediate behaviors, beyond the seeming functions of those behaviors, into the person. Many times there is a genetic disorder that has been missed, with an accompanying behavioral phenotype that spurs individuals to compulsively perform certain behaviors or to emit certain emotional responses. If we are busy trying to modify those behaviors and look at them as deliberate and manipulative, we are unable to help individuals learn to self-manage and deal with their own inherent tendencies. We are missing the forest for the trees and even missing the trees for the leaves. We are so focused on the manifestation of the syndrome that we cannot see the syndrome. We are so focused on changing and controlling people's behaviors that we miss the essence of who they are.

References

Allanson, J. E., Greenberg, F., & Smith, A. C. (1999). The face of Smith-Magenis syndrome: A subjective and objective study. *Journal of Medical Genetics, 36,* 394–397.

Fletcher, R., Loschen, E., Stavrakaki, C., & First, M. (Eds.). (2007). *DM–ID: A textbook of diagnosis of mental disorders in persons with intellectual disability.* Kingston, NY: NADD Press.

Parisi, M. A. (2009). Clinical and molecular features of Joubert syndrome and related disorders. *American Journal of Medical Genetics. Part C: Seminars in Medical Genetics, 15,* 326–340.

Williams, C. A. (2010). The behavioral phenotype of the Angelman syndrome. *American Journal of Medical Genetics, 154C,* 432–437.

Crack Babies, All Grown Up

Birth

It is Baltimore City, 1986. Inside an abandoned home, there are five people huddled together; they have just spent the last of their money on crack cocaine, and they are smoking it in a pipe. It is late fall. One woman in thin clothes has a protruding stomach. She is pregnant. Another has a small bump beneath her jeans. She is also pregnant but in her first trimester. They are huddled together around the pipe with one other woman and two men, all in equally threadbare clothes. A baby is crying in the background. That baby continues to cry, and no one pays any attention.

This was a common city scene in the 1980s during the crack-cocaine epidemic (Anderson, 1999). People lived, dealt drugs, even raised children in these abandoned homes, or crack houses, as they were often called. Aid to Families with Dependent Children was the welfare system in place at that time, which allotted money for mothers according to their need, based on the number of children they had. Mothers who were addicted to crack cocaine and in need of money could get financial assistance from the government by having babies: slightly more money, in fact, than working at an entry-level job. There was no financial support at that time for work training or community college programs.

During the mid-1980s, I worked in a shelter in the middle of Baltimore City. It was a shelter predominantly for women and children. Child after child came in with drug-addicted mothers. We called child protective services time and time again, describing signs of child abuse. But agency workers were unable to take the children unless they directly witnessed clear evidence of abuse. We watched as homeless children came and went with drug-addicted mothers who denied their addiction and treated their children as luggage at best, bad pets at worst. This was a horrifying time for me. But years later I met and began to work with many of these children as adults.

Developmental Delays

Babies weaned from crack were supposed not to have any developmental delays as a result of prenatal exposure to cocaine. Studies have repeatedly found no differences in IQ scores between groups of toddlers and preschoolers prenatally exposed to cocaine and those not exposed. One study found no differences in IQ scores at 24 months, measured using the Bayley Scales of Infant Development, between children exposed to cocaine prenatally and those not exposed (Frank, Augustyn, Knight, Pell, & Zukerman, 2001).

A large review of all the studies done with children 6 years old and under also revealed that no significant cognitive differences were found between children who had been prenatally exposed to cocaine and those who had not. Measures reviewed included teacher and parent behavioral reports, the Bayley Scale scores, and observational reports. These researchers concluded:

> Among children aged 6 years or younger, there is no convincing evidence that prenatal cocaine exposure is associated with developmental toxic effects that are different in severity, scope, or kind from the sequelae of multiple other risk factors. Many findings once thought to be specific effects of in utero cocaine exposure are correlated with other factors, including prenatal exposure to tobacco, marijuana, or alcohol, and the quality of the child's environment. (Frank et al., 2001, p. 1613)

For years, this was the assumption among researchers and clinicians: Babies with prenatal exposure to cocaine who may even have been born addicted to cocaine did not show any significant developmental delays as a result of the cocaine exposure. It was often assumed that any delays were more due to environment and exposure to alcohol and other toxic substances. Those small differences that were found, such as smaller head circumferences and lower birth weights, were regarded as largely insignificant and often resolved with development (Chasnoff, Griffith, Freier, & Murray, 1992).

It is important to note, however, that the validity of the Bayley Scales of Infant Development, used in those studies to measure children's IQ and to assess toddlers' development, has since been called into question by Hack et al. (2005). They concluded that the predictive validity of the Bayley Scales of Infant Development for cognitive functioning was poor. In other words, the scores ascertained, often showing little or no developmental delay, were not validated in testing given at older ages. Children not showing delays at age 2 or 3 could still show them later on, at 8 or 9 years of age. The predictive validity scores were not strong enough to assume that these children would not have significant delays in the future.

More recent studies have shown that prenatal exposure to cocaine, being in the uterus of a mother who was smoking crack, does cause developmental delays. Bennett, Bendersky, and Lewis (2008) did a broad study of exposed and nonexposed children at ages 4, 6, and 9 and concluded that "the findings indicate that cocaine exposure continues to place children at risk for mild cognitive deficits into preadolescence" (p. 919). One of their findings of interest was that boys had more impairment than girls. The areas of impairment were in abstract reasoning, visual reasoning, verbal reasoning, and short-term memory.

Potter, Zelazo, Stack, and Papageorgiou (2000) found that children who were prenatally exposed to cocaine had significantly impaired auditory-information processing abilities. This coincides with the conclusion reached by Chiriboga (1998), who found, in reviewing the older literature, that there was a common factor of inattentiveness that reoccurred in behavioral reports about children with prenatal cocaine exposure that was not present in children who had not been exposed.

Barik (2007) reported on possible reasons for the significantly higher incidence of heart problems found in children who had been exposed to cocaine as fetuses, due to possibly impaired organ development. In addition, these heart problems are likely to worsening with age. Below I describe the case histories of some of these children in order to begin to explore the implications for individuals with intellectual disability.

Effects of Prenatal Cocaine Exposure

Erin

In Chapter 1, I told the story of Kali, a young woman who was born addicted to crack and, with her mother, had been homeless as a baby. Kali had many emotional and psychological problems as a result of her upbringing and prenatal cocaine exposure. Before I met Kali, however, there was Erin. Erin's file indicated that her mother had abused crack cocaine while pregnant. Erin was a beautiful, bright, and humorous young woman—unless something she wanted didn't happen. Then Erin would run away and manage to travel for miles before anyone ever found her. She jumped out of vans and cars, sometimes into traffic. She worried us all, and no one could understand or anticipate her next move. She could be lovely, friendly, and kind, and then she would have a thought in her head and just run. The behavior plan that we had for her presented all kinds of incentives for staying put. She could earn shopping trips to buy the things she loved, such as jewelry, outfits, and shoes; she could do it all. Regardless of the incentives, she would still bolt. If anyone was ever rude or inattentive toward her, she might hit them (lightly) first and then run away. She could get away from anyone.

Erin was also very intelligent. She appeared capable of learning the skills necessary to get a job in the community. Staff attempted to work with her. However, she could not stay focused for more than 30 s. She would be talking about one topic, and 30 s later, as her companion began responding to the topic she had just brought up, she would already be talking about something entirely different. Staff became frustrated in their attempts to teach this very bright young woman. They began to complain that she was "uncooperative" and "noncompliant" because they knew she was smart and believed that she "knew better." In retrospect, it is likely that when their frustration began to show, she made her escape. She would often attempt to go home to her mother, where her sister lived but where she had been told, long ago, that she could not remain. Erin finally left us, only to bounce from community agency to community agency. Sometimes she was discharged, and at other times she signed herself out. She always appeared to be attempting to return home.

Sheena

Not only had Sheena's mother smoked crack when she was pregnant with Sheena; she was still smoking it—or whatever else happened to be available. Sheena had been in and out of foster and group homes and back and forth with Mom. Sheena reported that when she was at home, her mother had sometimes forced her to have sex with men coming in and out of the home in exchange for money for her mother to buy drugs. Sheena had also been molested and raped by several of her mother's boyfriends. (When Sheena first came to the community agency where I worked, she had been in an institutional setting for over a year. Within the first month, she jumped out the window and ran off to a waiting car driven by a young man whom she knew from years ago and who had recently gotten out of jail. She came back sometime the next day and left again two nights later. This time she went through the door after attacking and injuring the staff who tried to block her exit.

We were forced to tell staff to stop trying to block her, because we were committed to not using physical restraint and to making sure that both Sheena and the staff would not sustain any further injuries. Sheena came and went with one man after another and at the same time became engaged to a young man who served within the agency. Predictably, that was a tumultuous relationship. Sheena was intelligent, much like Erin, but was unable to focus on anything long enough to gain new skills for work situations. She also did not have a great deal of motivation to work. She found ways to get what she needed.

Sheena had a great deal of conflict with staff who wanted to use traditional methods to control her behavior. Even though her behavior plan had been changed and used only nontraditional methods, certain staff still tried to control her behavior through punishment and reward. This only made her angry and spurred her on to engage in constant conflict with these staff. Also, much like Kali, whenever she was close to earning a traditional reward, she would somehow sabotage her own success. This happened again and again until we finally convinced staff in the home that she should not have to earn rewards but should have positive outcomes in her life on a noncontingent basis and losses that were based only on natural consequences. The more this approach was implemented, the more Sheena stopped engaging in power struggles with her staff and stopped sabotaging herself as well.

Sheena and Erin both exhibited a severe form of attention deficit disorder (ADD) that did not respond to medication. They also exhibited difficulties with impulse control. Both were on a great deal of medication, but it was difficult to determine the effectiveness of that medication on their impulses because no psychiatrist wanted to do the experiment of reducing the medication in significant quantities. Minor adjustments were the most that could be expected. But this pattern that I began to observe, of severe ADD and damaged executive functioning as demonstrated by both impulse control problems and short-term memory difficulties, repeated itself as I got to know more young adults who had been prenatally damaged by crack cocaine.

PrenatalCocaine Exposure and Severe Impulsivity

John

A young man came to the agency around this same time. John's mother admitted to having had a serious crack problem and having abused crack while pregnant. She had since gotten treatment and was doing very well in her life. She was very committed to her son and took him home to visit often. John was severely intellectually disabled and had a seizure disorder. His impulse control disorder was so extreme that he would jump out of moving cars and run into traffic if he became upset with staff, run away, and attack staff both at his residence and at the day program, sometimes inflicting serious injury. John had a more involved disability than we had seen before. He sometimes believed that he was a superhero and would act out the role of his favorite character. His behavior was much like a pinball inside an old-fashioned pinball table. He did not respond to traditional behavioral programming and was unable to focus on whatever incentive was being presented: No matter how brief the time span in which he could earn it, he would forget about it and move on to the next stimuli. He was easily redirected, however. But when a desire was thwarted, he could become explosive within moments.

It almost appeared as though the crack cocaine had affected John's executive functioning much in the way that a frontal lobe head injury would. He had no filter for impulses; words and actions would tumble forward. In addition, he would respond to any stimulation, no matter how small or large, in much the same way.

The behavior plan in place for John sought to remove stimuli that were thought to set off John's behaviors: his favorite TV shows and toys pertaining to that show. The result was protracted power struggles between John and the staff: John would still find ways to play with, and talk about, his favorite action figures from the show, including drawing them. When staff tried to remove the toys or even the pictures, John would become angry and attack staff.

The behavior plan only caused a negative cycle and power struggle. Staff finally gave up and let John enjoy his toys, redirecting him only when he was overly agitated in play. When John realized that staff were no longer trying to restrict and control him, he calmed down and actually became far more cooperative. Behavior plans targeting noncompliance with people who have impulse control issues often frustrate them further and actually increase noncompliance due to the level of frustration they are experiencing.

It was wonderful that staff, on their own, convinced the psychology associate who wrote the plan to change it. I had not been successful in doing this. John had some wonderful months before, sadly, he died as a result of suffocation during a severe seizure. At his funeral, we were surprised to see all the church and family members whose lives he had touched. Many people spoke of their love for John. Those who were not so concerned about John's negative behaviors were quickly able to discover and connect with the wonderful person that John truly was.

The Impact of Fetal Alcohol and Cocaine Exposure

Lisa B.

Women who smoke crack cocaine during pregnancy often drink as well. The combination of crack and alcohol exposure creates a unique profile. Lisa B. was one such case. She had been adopted at a very young age by two wonderful and very caring people. However, by age 12 she was out of control. At age 14 she was placed in a residential facility after repeatedly attacking her mother. Despite a calm and nurturing upbringing, she had many behavioral problems. When she came to our agency, she was in her mid-20s and had been unsuccessful in all of her previous placements.

Lisa B. was not able to take responsibility for her actions. No matter what she had said or done, she could not see how she had created, quite directly at times, her current predicament. Instead, she was convinced that she was being victimized or that she was an innocent bystander; that was the missing neuronal link between cause and effect created by the alcohol. She also had a hard time controlling her impulses. Once she had a thought, she had to act on it. As a result, she smoked two packs of cigarettes a day and weighed almost 400 pounds. She had a very difficult time with self-control because the impulse would hit her to eat or drink, but she could not see how her actions directly related to her weight gain. Rewards for weight loss were all too long term to assist her in not acting on impulses. Punishment, or losing a reward, made her angry, of course, and when angry she acted on her negative impulses, sometimes becoming aggressive.

Lisa was in a negative cycle that was hard to break. Another of her impulses was to go to the hospital, where attention was abundant and meals and snacks flowed ceaselessly. The part of her brain responsible for figuring out routes worked well, and she had learned to call 911 to say she wanted to hurt herself. Whenever she felt deprived of attention or food or both, this was her first impulse. When, as punishment, her phone was removed for month-long increments, she found new ways to make the calls, including borrowing neighbors' phones. Rewards for not going to the hospital could not compete with her impulse to be in the haven of food and attention.

The only intervention that succeeded in breaking Lisa's pattern of biweekly hospital visits was finding her a meaningful work placement. She found that she played a role at her workplace, of helping individuals with intellectual disability more severe than hers, and she found meaning in that role.

This was not a reward held over her head. Instead, it was a role she played where she was genuinely helpful and, after a while, truly needed. Lisa B. never stopped going to the hospital completely, but she vastly reduced her attempts, going several times a year rather than several times a month. The behavior plan did not work; the many rewards offered for activities and items she enjoyed and even cared about were insufficient. What was sufficient was a realistic role she could play in which she was actually helpful each day to another person and genuinely needed. This sense of importance and of purpose was all that helped her. She naturally ate and smoked less when she was busy helping people at her job. A positive cycle was begun.

Anthony

Anthony also demonstrated a profile of mixed prenatal cocaine and alcohol exposure. Anthony had the facial features of someone with fetal alcohol syndrome, and indeed his mother had admitted to drinking while pregnant. However, Anthony also had a severe impulse control problem and was unable to focus or attend for very long on any one stimulus. I did not understand Anthony's profile at the time that I worked with him. I thought that he might have had an undetected head injury, and I grilled him about accidents, falls, and so on. At that time, I did not realize the full impact of fetal cocaine exposure.

Anthony had an intellectual disability. He also had a criminal record and a long list of charges. He repeatedly stole items when the opportunity presented itself. He never planned his thefts, stealing only by impulse. He would become aggressive at times when his intent was frustrated. He could be pleasant one minute and completely enraged the next. His profile so resembled a person with a head injury that I could not be convinced that he did not have one. At the work program, staff would try to teach him new skills, and although he could do repetitive skills well, he could not focus well enough to learn a higher level of skill. In addition to impulsive acts of theft and aggression, Anthony never admitted guilt, even when caught. There was always a long story about how he had no choice but to commit the questionable act. He even tried to explain a rape in that manner. He is now incarcerated, unfortunately.

In retrospect, I understand that Anthony's cognitive damage from fetal alcohol syndrome was what caused him not to be able to take full responsibility for his actions, while his impulse control difficulties resulting from prenatal cocaine exposure led him to act on impulse, without reflection on the consequences of his actions, often violating the rights of others in the process. Finally, he could not attend well enough to learn a new way of operating and new skills as a result of the cocaine exposure. He relied on the street skills with which he had grown up, having been raised by parents who were also in and out of jail. He could not learn a new set of skills, nor could he process the negative effects of those he had been using. Regardless of the services offered to him, he still ended up in the criminal justice system, where he will be incarcerated for a very long time.

Sadly, one might reflect that there are probably many individuals currently incarcerated who were also exposed prenatally to a combination of alcohol and drugs. The lack of ability to process cause and effect, along with impulse control and attentional difficulties, certainly sets the stage for criminal activity, particularly if the individual was exposed to such activity while growing up. A vicious cycle ensues.

Anthony had a behavior plan that targeted aggression and theft. This helped only in a mild way, to control the environment. Anthony could maintain focus or the willpower to earn rewards. When temptation was present, such as an available wallet, he could not resist. Due to the difficulties he had with executive functioning, he did not think then of the reward he could earn for not stealing at the crucial moment. Nor, when someone made him angry and staff were attempting to redirect or block him, did he think about the consequences of attacking others. Anthony's brain was damaged in a way that made it difficult to avoid criminal activities that he had been brought up to view as normal. He could not reason his way past his negative upbringing or reason his way toward taking responsibility for his actions. The damage done to his brain by the combined alcohol and cocaine damage left him almost helpless against his negative impulses.

In retrospect, if Anthony were in my care today, I would try very hard to find a meaningful role for him to play in his life. I would search for a girlfriend, a job, a role within the home—anything to redirect and reframe his impulses and give him a sense of purpose and belonging. Rather than creating an elaborate plan with different rewards and consequences, I would focus on searching for a meaningful role through which Anthony could see himself in another light completely. In this way, he might have changed his behavior by rising to his vision of himself, rather than going with the impulses that arose moment to moment. As he committed more and more illegal acts, his view of himself as a criminal was solidified, though he had no understanding of how his actions had created this role and how it could have been undone.

Summary

Nichiren Daishonin, A Buddhist teacher from 13th-century Japan, once stated: "If you try to treat someone's illness without knowing its cause, you will only make the person sicker than before" (p. 774). That is what we, as psychologists in the disability community, have been trying to do. We apply behavioral principles to issues that are not behavioral in nature. We treat brain damage with sticks and carrots rather than with therapeutic treatment. But what we need to do is to teach coping strategies so that individuals can learn to compensate for the damaged areas of their brain. We need to help them to find a meaningful role in society and a place in the social world where they belong. We need to help them to see themselves as valuable and their own lives as meaningful. Finally, we ourselves need to value them in order to teach them to value themselves. If we see past the behaviors into the whole person, past the damage into the heart of the human being behind it, then we can have the insight needed to help these individuals find a meaningful role in the world. It all begins with us.

References

Anderson, E. (1999). *Code of the street*. New York: W. W. Norton.

Barik, S. (2007). The thrill can kill: Murder by methylation. *Molecular Pharmacology, 71,* 1203–1205.

Bennett, D. S., Bendersky, M., & Lewis, M. (2008). Children's cognitive ability from 4 to 9 years old as a function of prenatal cocaine exposure, environmental risk, and maternal verbal intelligence. *Developmental Psychology, 44,* 919–928.

Chasnoff, I. S., Griffith, D. R., Freier, C., & Murray, J. (1992). Cocaine/polydrug use in pregnancy: Two-year follow-up. *Pediatrics, 89,* 284–289.

Chiriboga, C. A. (1998). Neurobiological correlates of fetal cocaine exposure. *Annals of the New York Academy of Sciences, 846,* 109–125.

Daishonin, N. (1999). *Major writings of Nichiren Daishonin* (Compilation). Tokyo: Nichiren Shoshu International Center. (Original work published in 13th century)

Frank, D. A., Augustyn, M., Knight, W. G., Pell, T., & Zukerman, B. (2001). Growth, development, and behavior in early childhood following prenatal cocaine exposure: A systematic review. *Journal of the American Medical Association, 285,* 1613–1625.

Hack, M., Taylor, H. G., Drotar, D., Schluchter, M., Cartar, L., Wilson-Costello, D., & Morrow, M. (2005). Poor predictive validity of the Bayley Scales of Infant Development for cognitive function of extremely low birth weight children at school age. *Pediatrics, 116,* 333–341.

Potter, S. M., Zelazo, P. R., Stack, D. M., & Papageorgiou, A. N. (2000). Adverse effects of fetal cocaine exposure on neonatal auditory information processing. *Pediatrics, 105,* 40.

The Truth about Trauma

In the 25 years that I have practiced psychology in the field of intellectual disability, I have come to firmly believe that approximately 90% of the behavioral issues that I have seen have actually been trauma-based responses. Of the remainder, 5% have been full-blown psychiatric disorders, and another 5% have fit the American Behavioral Association model of behaviors designed by the individual to produce a given response.

Why? The reason is because trauma is pervasive in the lives of individuals with intellectual disability. It is traumatic to be excluded from the very first day in kindergarten throughout all years of school from the normal school experience and class work. In addition, many individuals with ID faced merciless ridicule by fellow students. Many individuals were rejected by their own family due to their disability. Many were placed in foster care in which the care was questionable. Many were raised by families with drug and alcohol problems—the same problems that produced the disability in the first place. Many individuals with ID were sexually and physically abused while growing up and/or as adults. Dave Hinsberger (1987), an expert on sexual abuse in individuals with ID, estimates, based on his research, that 8 of 10 females and 6 of 10 males in this population have been sexually abused.

Antecedents or Triggers

Behavioral responses and trauma-based responses can look very similar: They both may appear to be responses to an antecedent. Trauma-based responses appear to be caused by an antecedent because they are actual fight-or-flight reactions of the sympathetic nervous system, which was triggered by an event. This event can look like an antecedent, and it can appear as though the response was calculated. However, the truth is that there is implicit memory stored within each of us, and a reminder in the environment can trigger emotional responses. These emotional responses can be based on implicit or basically unconscious memories. We might not remember that a big dog once bit us, but still we become tense and move away when we are around big dogs.

Our bodies remember. When Denny, whom we met in Chapter 1, came out of the institution, he began flipping table and chairs every time he saw someone with straight blond hair. He likely had an implicit or stored memory of an abusive situation or series of abusive situations at the hands of someone with straight blond hair.

Fight, Flight, or Freeze Responses

The human brain has three basic layers, reflecting the evolution of the species (Howard, 2000). The first level, centering on the brainstem region, controls the mechanisms whereby our bodies respond to reflex stimulation. This reflects our days as reptiles and amphibians. Next, our animal brain, or limbic system, comprises the sympathetic and parasympathetic systems, which served the species well in its days of animalistic living. The limbic system enabled us to move rapidly, when danger appeared, from a state of calm into fight, flight, or freeze mode, depending on what the situation called for: attacking, defending, fleeing, or playing dead. Finally, the higher-level brain controls abstract thought and executive functioning, such as decision making and negotiating our way through an uncertain world. This is where our rational thinking lies.

If we think about individuals with ID, we can see that they often are responding in fear during a behavioral incident. They may actually be in fight, flight, or freeze mode, with a highly stimulated sympathetic nervous system. What are they stimulated by? A sense of danger.

Danger can be based on the perception that one might be attacked, on the perception of loss or deprivation or of being deceived, or on the perception of the threat of physical or sexual abuse. All of these perceptions might trigger the sympathetic nervous system into taking over the brain. At that point, all the individual can think about is either fighting, fleeing, or freezing. The rational mind is completely overpowered by the panic mode of the sympathetic nervous system. All of us have seen people in this mode: They are not trying to procure a certain outcome; they are trying, instead, to protect themselves from the danger. The trigger is not an antecedent that lets them know that they might get something that they want; it is actually a sign that they are in some kind of danger or perceived danger.

We have also seen people freeze. Many individuals with ID freeze when triggered or overcome by fear. It has been my experience that certain individuals, when feeling threatened, will appear to be less cognitively aware than they actually are. I have worked with a number of people who "hid" from those whom they found threatening by appearing unaware. For example, people in more traditional day programs surrounded by somewhat agitated individuals or somewhat threatening staff might pretend to be lower functioning or less aware and cognitively capable than they actually are in order to stay out of the line of fire, so to speak. I have had the experience of working with countless individuals who revealed far more cognitive abilities when they were in a safe setting than they otherwise revealed in their normal day and residential settings. This is a form of freezing.

Shutting down and refusing to interact is another form of freezing. A threatened animal might attempt to play dead; threatened individuals who believe themselves to be powerless may shut down and refuse to interact. I have been called in to write behavior plans for individuals in response to what staff termed noncompliance only to find people who were scared out of their minds and trying to avoid danger.

Trauma Mind

Mary Jo Barrett (2010) has elaborated a theory about the "trauma mind" in reference to individuals with PTSD. While in trauma mind, the individual is in fight-or-flight mode. In addition, the individual regresses to the age at which he or she was traumatized mentally. So if, for example, there is a man with intellectual disability who was traumatized by physical abuse at ages 2, 3, and 4 and then subsequently taken from his home, later in life, when he feels in danger, he will revert to fight-or-flight mode and go into his trauma mind. That mind will be of a 2-, 3-, or 4-year-old, even though the individual has the body of a 40-year-old. Then that 40-year-old will respond as a 3- or 4-year-old—maybe lashing out against the source of perceived danger or trying to flee—depending on his nature and response habits from years of PTSD.

Trauma mind is an interesting concept because it demonstrates how one's state of mind totally changes when responding in the fight-or-flight mode. The trauma mind is a state of mind in which one regresses to the time of the trauma and does not think in an adult-like or rational manner. Those aspects of our mind no longer function when we are in trauma mind.

Those of us who have worked with individuals with behavioral problems understand this state of mind. Many of the behaviorally involved people with whom we work seem to regress significantly while acting out. Although we may remind them of the consequences of their acts, those reminders have absolutely no impact. Staff often tell me this. And it is because the individual has gone into a different state of mind, having regressed to the time of an earlier trauma and responding irrationally in a fight-or-flight mode.

Let's return to Denny as an example.

Denny

Denny was in fight-or-flight mode, and he clearly regressed every time he saw the woman who looked like the person who had abused him. His behavior would change dramatically when he saw her: From a state of complete calm he would then start throwing objects and flipping tables. He became a child responding in panic to protect himself. He had, in fact, been placed at the institution as a young child and was very likely repeatedly traumatized during that placement. Just losing family and being in a situation of one staff to 10 or even 15 children was likely traumatic, let alone conditions within the institution that he must have experienced as a child. No incentive motivated him to stop throwing chairs and flipping tables. He was not able to link his response with an outcome rationally. He was in fight-or-flight mode, triggered and trying to stop impending danger.

Many acts of aggression that I have witnessed through the years appear to have actually been the panicked fight-or-flight responses of individuals with ID who had perceived a danger. We always wondered why the incentives never worked and why the antecedents did not appear provocative. Now I realize that the majority of the people for whom I wrote behavior plans had experienced trauma and were in trauma mind when performing irrational behaviors.

Implicit Versus Explicit Memory

In *The Mindful Therapist,* Dan Siegel (2010) wrote about trauma in terms of implicit versus explicit memory. The implicit memory contains emotional memories and is not called forth in a rational manner. Those memories can pop up at any time and can even appear as though they are occurring in the present. A good example is when we smell a scent and feel as though we are in a place we had been years ago when we smelled that same scent, like Grandma's kitchen or the kindergarten classroom. These memories are not encoded or called forth by the conscious mind; they just occur.

Conversely, explicit memory is specifically called up based on the conscious mind activating the retrieval process. It is encoded material, like the name of the school where we attended kindergarten or the town in which Grandma lived. It is factual and autobiographical.

When we respond in trauma mode, we do not call up this explicit memory and say to ourselves, "someone hurt me once and now I feel as though someone might hurt me again and so I am becoming upset." We are often flooded with implicit memories that know no time and feel as though they are presently occurring. The emotions themselves are part of the memory and come back to us without being consciously called. Instead they are triggered. Therefore, they overtake us with emotion, and we begin to respond in ways that we had not planned, ways that are not always rational. We manifest a sympathetic nervous system and may even sweat or breathe rapidly. The same process occurs with adults with ID. They are flooded with feelings that have been triggered, not consciously pulled up. They respond irrationally, and they manifest physical changes, such as breathing hard, turning red, and talking rapidly or stuttering. This cannot be viewed as a calculated behavior when it is obvious that implicit memories are activated and a fight-or-flight response is what is driving the behavior manifested. Even when the response does not seem warranted or, rather, particularly when the response does not seem warranted, implicit memory, usually of some level of past trauma, is being activated.

Paul

Paul was born to a mother living on the streets of a poor South American country. She was alleged to have had a serious drug problem. He spent his first 3 years going back and forth between his mother and grandmother's home. His mother was frequently homeless. He would live on the street with her for a while and then go back with his grandmother and his grandmother's boyfriend. At age 3, Paul was found in the grandmother's home with over 35 cigar burns on his body. There was also reported sexual abuse from the grandmother's boyfriend. Upon the discovery of Paul's condition, he was taken from the home and adopted by a family in the United States. Paul had a sister who was also taken. Their adopted family raised them both with love and care.

The sister did not have cognitive damage and was able to adjust to her new life. Paul, however, had incidents of attempting to touch other children sexually throughout childhood. He also received special education services because of the brain damage due to fetal exposure to drugs and alcohol. Paul had problems with explosive anger and had difficulties paying attention; it appeared as though he had endured fetal cocaine exposure. Paul had difficulties with sexually inappropriate behaviors and aggression throughout childhood. He had a variety of residential and day placements. However, he continued to have difficulties and to act on impulses.

From the previous chapter, we know that Paul suffered with the signs and symptoms of many adult children with fetal cocaine exposure. Paul also experienced the trauma of prolonged hunger and physical and sexual abuse in the first 3 years of his life. This early childhood trauma had a tremendous impact on Paul. At a meeting in a community placement setting held for Paul, the staff complained bitterly about him: "He eats constantly, he tries to take money from more defenseless residents, he also tries to get people to give him their snacks at work. He is a bully. All he wants is everyone else's stuff. He needs consequences. He knows better."

Almost everyone at Paul's annual meeting was upset with him. He had already had several behavior plans, and the staff complained that he needed to lose more privileges and understand the consequences of his actions. Even the most sincere people were expressing frustration with this young adult who seemed insatiable in his need. He was also periodically explosive but had recently been so medicated at his last hospitalization that he could no longer be so volatile. His hunger and thirst, however, had increased even more due to the medication that he received, and he was begging and bullying even more for drinks and snacks.

"His problems are behavioral!" the team agreed. They turned to me to improve the behavior plan and address his bullying and manipulating. My response was to point out that the medications were making his hunger and thirst worse. We planned to continue working with the psychiatrist to reduce medication. Staff were not satisfied, however. They felt he was deliberate in his greed and need.

Paul felt constantly in need because he had been constantly hungry and thirsty in his most formative and developmentally important years (0–3). The trauma of being deprived and going without never left him. He felt, from that point forward, that he could never get enough. He had a continuous need to procure more and more. He would stockpile food supplies in his room. He obviously feared the day he would, again, be deprived of food. The implicit memories of being deprived were deeply ingrained in his subconscious mind. The fear of being deprived again drove him to beg and bully. On top of the traumatic memories and fears that dominated his psyche, the medications that were supposed to help his psychological unrest actually heightened his sensations of thirst and hunger. He was caught in a vicious cycle.

In addition, Paul smoked, but staff would not allow him to bring cigarettes to work. We discovered this at his annual meeting. Of course, not having cigarettes when his co-workers did only increased his sense of deprivation, and he impulsively begged and bullied for money and cigarettes while around others. Paul was constantly triggered into fight-or-flight mode by the feeling of not having enough and his implicit memories of deprivation. He got into fights with people over his begging for money, snacks, and cigarettes. Instead of understanding his base of trauma and the triggers that occurred when he felt deprived and experienced those implicit memories, staff labeled him a bully and increased the restrictions on his access to these things. The increased restrictions made Paul feel more deprived and only increased the begging and bullying.

Instead of consenting to a behavior plan with more consequences as staff requested, I was able to reinitiate therapy. Paul desperately needed trauma work in a serious therapeutic setting. He is currently receiving eye movement desensitization and reprocessing therapy (EMDR) and seeing a therapist weekly. He has more supplies during the day and is not so panicked about being hungry, thus causing him to feel safe and act more calmly throughout the day. In addition, his medications have been significantly reduced.

Often people with severe trauma are diagnosed as having bipolar disorders because sleepless nights and severe mood swings are part of their PTSD. This was the case with Paul. Being taken off the medications targeting the bipolar factor helped him to reduce his level of physiological sensations of hunger and thirst. The therapy and antidepressants helped to improve and stabilize his overall mood. He is now doing better and, we hope, will continue to improve his ability to enjoy his life each day.

Big Ts and Little ts

Francine Shapiro (2001), the innovator of EMDR and an overall pioneer in the field of trauma treatment, introduced the concepts of "big T trauma" and "little t trauma." Big T trauma applies to what we ordinarily think of as trauma: rape, molestation, physical abuse, car accidents, disasters, and so on. We are all familiar with the impact of the big *T*s. Little *t*s, however, are the small events that cause pain but do not seem significant in the eyes of others: for example, being humiliated in front of a group of people in some way but not physically hurt or abused.

These little *t*s add up, according to Shapiro, and create their own brand of PTSD. Think, for a moment, about the lives of individuals who have an intellectual disability. They are continually reminded that they are different from others in the course of their daily lives. Throughout school they may be pointed at, laughed at, sometimes even called names. Although this may not appear to be abuse, it has the same effect. If you think of an embarrassing moment and then imagine having one almost every single day in some form or another, that adds up to a great deal of pain. Imagine bearing that pain day in and day out. That is the normal state of many with ID. Little *t*s accumulate and sometimes have as big an impact as a big *T* trauma.

Individuals with ID are likely to have many little *t* and big *T* trauma experiences. They are even more likely to be carrying the effects of those experiences with them and not to have had anyone to talk it over or process the effects with. Many are carrying emotional burdens that may seem like hundreds of pounds of heavy weight on their shoulders and may cause periodic outbursts when inadvertently triggered. These outbursts may seem like purely behavioral incidents but are actually trauma-based responses. By *trauma-based,* I mean triggered by an event that stirs an implicit memory and provokes an emotional response.

Frequently we do not know why someone with ID is responding in the way that he or she is, and we conclude that this behavior is manipulative or intended to produce a certain outcome. In fact, it may be trauma based, and even if the trauma was only a little *t* trauma, it may have evoked emotions that are now spilling forth through a behavioral incident. An indicator that this may be occurring is often the overreaction.

Staff will often tell me that they did not know or understand why some individuals responded the way that they did because the response was much more intense than was warranted by the situation. The overreaction can indicate the presence of a fight-or-flight response to a triggered implicit memory. In other words, if people overreact behaviorally, it is likely that they are exhibiting trauma-based responses rather than purely behavioral responses. This is particularly true if an overreaction was triggered by a specific environmental factor or event.

Trauma of Invalidation

A very important little *t* trauma is what I would like to call the "trauma of invalidation." Many of us may remember as children when we had a certain feeling but were told by adults that we didn't actually feel that way. "Oh you are fine," many a depressed or traumatized child was told. "That little boy didn't mean to hurt you. You shouldn't be angry," a mother may tell her child when the child clearly knows that the little boy in question was very deliberately on the attack. We are told that we do not understand, that we are not hurt, that we should not be angry, and so on. But as we grow up and take our place in society as adults, we are able to assert our feelings and perceptions more effectively and validate ourselves. We are then validated by the social environment as well.

Individuals with ID often do not have this experience. They are often not validated for the feelings that they express. They are sometimes told, when coworkers or housemates are abusive toward them, that they are not being abused. They just have to ignore the person. Or they are told not to worry because the person has a behavior plan. Or they are just instructed on how to calm down rather than listened to about the cause of their anger or emotional distress. These are all ways in which people with ID are made to feel that their emotions and responses are not valid.

Many times individuals with ID express repeatedly that they wish to change jobs. Over and over again they are either told that the topic will be discussed at a meeting; in some cases, the meeting is almost a year away. "We will talk about changing jobs at your annual meeting," many persons with a disability have been told when complaining about a job or day program placement. Or, "You like it just fine on Fridays when we have movie day," and so on. Imagine, for a moment, that you have a job that you hate. Try as you might to quit, even though you know there are other jobs that are available to you, you are unable to quit. (Though some readers may, in fact, feel that they are in such a situation, those of us without disabilities do have the ability to quit, regardless of other constraints.) Many people with ID do not like where they live and who they live with; yet they may be told by staff that they actually do like it. Their feelings of dislike are even invalidated. This may not seem traumatic, but the accumulated result of being invalidated day after day, year after year, can actually be quite traumatic. Little *t* traumas add up and sometimes have a big *T* impact.

Trauma-Based Responses

Judith Herman (1997) identified three main emotional outcomes of trauma in her book, *Trauma and Recovery:* feelings of powerlessness, feelings of being disconnected, and a lack of a sense of safety. Her book is a defining work in the field of trauma, pinpointing the effects of trauma and the clear symptoms of PTSD. She clearly instructs the therapist working with individuals with trauma to address these three areas; treatment cannot be effective otherwise. Below I discuss these three areas in the context of individuals with ID.

Power

Individuals with ID are almost defined by their powerlessness. The choices they have in their housing arrangements, daily work, and even relationships with others are often minimal. Many agencies serving individuals with ID give lip service to the concept of choice, but the actual implementation is somewhat lacking. People with ID don't usually even choose the agencies that house them and work with them. The power they have to change their lives often lies in their ability to advocate for themselves. Some people are not very good self-advocates. Some people cannot speak well or at all. Others cannot feel hopeful enough even to attempt to request a change in their lives. Yet others who speak well and can request changes are largely ignored due to their lack of power. Having no power is a state of life when you have an intellectual disability.

Consider, in addition to the challenges presented above, individuals who have been sexually or physically abused. Through this abuse, they have come to see themselves as persons who can be the target of others' physical and sexual aggression. They are unable to stop the abuse, which at the time rendered them powerless, and may continue to see themselves as unable to have an effect on their own lives. They may even see themselves as persons who are likely to be abused again and who may even deserve it, depending on what emotional messages were given them along with the physical and sexual abuse.

Laney is an individual with fetal alcohol syndrome who was repeatedly sexually abused by her stepfather. Laney resides in an agency and lives with people whom she does not like. She often has some form of sex on the van ride to and from work and in other inappropriate situations. She is eager to please whomever might want sexual favors from her. Laney does not see herself as being able to change her living situation or to say no to the individuals who grope her daily.

Laney actually understands her worth as a sexual object. A behavior plan is written for Laney, in which she is rewarded for not being promiscuous, and yet it does not work because she does not feel empowered to say no to the men who have been accustomed to engaging in sexual acts with Laney on the van and in other settings. She cannot change any aspect of her behavior until she is empowered. This is yet another true scenario with the name changed. Eventually Laney was finally able to settle down and date one person at a time after receiving therapy that was trauma focused and included EMDR to address the trauma from the years of sexual abuse.

Sometimes bullying and generally aggressive behavior can be an expression of powerlessness. Some individuals may feel as though the only way they can get their sense of power back is to attack those who have even less power than themselves. This kind of negative chain can be witnessed in certain settings where there is little supervision and individuals are not given choices or the leeway to move about freely and select the activities they wish to engage in. There is no excuse for bullying, but it is often the expression of powerlessness and the associated frustration.

Disconnection

Feelings of being disconnected or being unable to build meaningful connections with others is, according to Herman (2007), a primary effect of trauma. Trauma causes one to lose trust in others and to be unable to bond with others accordingly. Individuals with ID are already isolated and alienated from the majority of the population as a result of their disability. From Day 1 in the school system, they are often placed in a separate classroom, isolated, segregated, and set away from others. As life progresses, they are kept from many mainstream activities, such as driving, dating, working summer jobs, and so on. This isolation in lifestyle leads to isolation from relationships. Experiences of isolation and alienation may become little *t* traumas as they accumulate. For the individual with ID who has accumulated experiences of being left out, rejected, and excluded, one more exclusion could become the trigger that releases a fight-or-flight response.

Lack of Safety

In Chapter 1, we met Charles, an individual who had been repeatedly abused in psychiatric settings. I had been doing therapy with Charles for a few months when he made the suicide attempt I described earlier. That attempt was in response to the restriction that had been placed on him. Charles felt completely powerless when he was told he could not smoke and, as a result, attempted to take his own life. He was connected to no one and, in his despair, expressed himself through that attempt. A few months earlier he had been in the waiting room of our clinic when I heard screaming. I came out of my office only to find Charles huddled in a corner, shaking. I asked him what was wrong. Charles pointed to a staff person who was there with another individual with ID. "It's him! It's him!" he screamed. We had to remove this staff person from the waiting room immediately and make sure that Charles was nowhere near him. Slowly, Charles stood up and returned to his chair after about 15 min. He was still shaking.

Eventually we learned that the staff member looked just like someone who was abusive to Charles at a state hospital. Charles was convinced that it was the same person, and as he hadn't felt safe anywhere near that staff person in the hospital, the same was true when he thought he had encountered his abuser in the clinic waiting room. The implicit memory of horrible abuse had been triggered. Charles was in fight-or-flight mode and tried his best to escape into a corner of the room. It took a long, long time to comfort him. An important part of comforting him was helping him to feel grounded in the present. He believed he was back at the hospital and at the mercy of sadistic staff. We were finally able to bring him back to the here and now, and he was able to relax. His session was, nevertheless, an outpouring of the abuse that had occurred. Many individuals with ID in state psychiatric hospitals have endured horrible abuse from other patients who did not have ID. Charles later shared these experiences also. We had to make sure that Charles never again encountered that staff person. We also had to make sure that he never lived with residents who had aggressive tendencies. Charles rarely felt safe in his life, and we had to work to do as much as we could to help him to have that sense. Obviously, as proven by the later suicide attempt, we did not do a very good job. Now he is living with staff he feels safe with far away from his previous setting. He has two docile and caring housemates and is on the long road to recovery.

I have repeatedly witnessed unrelated and repeated behavioral incidents from individuals who did not feel safe in their own homes. There are a variety of reasons why people with ID might not feel safe: housemates who have bullying tendencies, staff who are not engaged or predictable in their actions, visitors who are not expected and known, such as friends of staff and even administrators who visit and provoke anxious responses from the staff.

One woman whom I counseled became psychotic, although she had been stable for several years. Trudy began yelling, attacked her very docile housemate, and threatened staff with a knife. Trudy was then hospitalized. She stabilized in the hospital, was released, and went home. Once at home she became psychotic again, responding to voices she appeared to be hearing, threatening staff, and trying to hurt both staff and her housemates. She was rehospitalized again. This cycle continued over a 4-month period with four separate hospitalizations. Finally, the truth came out. A weekend staff member had an abusive husband who was coming over and getting into altercations with his wife. The residents were witnessing their fights. Trudy had been repeatedly triggered and possibly retraumatized by the altercations and the apparent threats that this man had been making toward his wife. The wife, of course, tried to hide that this was occurring at the residence. Trudy's psychosis was, in fact, a trauma response. She felt safe in the hospital and was thus able to regain her calm there. As soon as she reentered the home, however, she again felt unsafe and would demonstrate a fight-or-flight response. Trudy finally became stable when she was placed in another home. Even though that staff member was removed and her husband never returned, Trudy continued to have behavioral difficulties at that home. When she moved to another home, she finally felt safe.

The importance of safety, particularly for individuals with ID who have experienced both big *T* and little *t* trauma cannot be emphasized enough. Individuals cannot begin the recovery process if they do not feel safe in their own homes. Trauma responses are more likely to be triggered, and fight or flight is the form they take. Many times I have been told about an individual with ID who chronically runs away, only to find that that individual was being threatened in some way by another resident or staff within the home. I have also found that people with ID who have excessive restrictions in the home also attempt flight. Restrictions can act as triggers by provoking implicit memories of neglect and abandonment. Part of feeling safe is knowing that basic needs can be met, that there is no threat of harm, and that there is someone who will listen. These basic criteria are not met for many individuals with ID in institutional and community living situations. This explains a great many of the behavioral problems staff cite in these individuals. When people don't feel safe, they don't always act rationally. Fight, flight, or freeze is triggered through a sense of danger. Trauma responses are triggered through fear.

Developmental Trauma Disorder

Van der Kolk, McFarlane, and Weisaeth (2007) have proposed that a new diagnosis, of "developmental trauma disorder," be used for children and adolescents exposed to abuse and neglect. Van der Kolk et al. asserted that childhood trauma can cause learning disabilities, cognitive impairments, mental health problems, and behavioral issues that not only present in childhood but carry on throughout life. This may, indeed, be the correct diagnosis for many individuals with ID. Cognitive difficulties may even result from trauma—thus, the diagnosis of ID. One of the categories that Van der Kolk (2010) proposed on his Web site as a criterion for developmental trauma disorder is functional impairment, which includes intellectual impairment. Functional impairment is defined as follows:

> The disturbance causes clinically significant distress or impairment in at least two of the following areas of functioning:
> • Scholastic: under-performance, non-attendance, disciplinary problems, drop-out, failure to complete degree/credential(s), conflict with school personnel, learning disabilities or intellectual impairment that cannot be accounted for by neurological or other factors.

Those of us who have worked with individuals with ID and a history of a great deal of trauma are often shocked by the level of cognitive ability we see glimpses of when the individuals are in a relaxed state. It may very well be that as individuals feel safe and begin to recover from previous trauma, they begin to function better cognitively as well. This also raises the question of whether certain individuals with ID would still have been diagnosed with ID if they had not had repeated trauma experience.

Trauma is pervasive in the world of individuals with ID. Abuse, neglect, sexual abuse, and other big *T* traumas abound in the lives of many individuals with ID. Many have ID because of fetal exposure to alcohol or drugs. It becomes a chicken-or-the-egg issue for many, as it can be difficult to pinpoint cause and effect: Did the trauma they grew up with decrease their intellectual functioning, or did the womb they were raised in subject them to brain damage? The environments they are raised in after birth can be as destructive as the drug- and alcohol-soaked wombs that housed them early on.

Van der Kolk (2010) illustrated the vicious cycle that ensues when the initial bond that a child has to the caregiver is not strong and there is little or no emotional support. That child cannot develop a sense of security, and quite often the child is removed from the home. This trauma of attachment problems creates patterns in individuals at early ages that may manifest later in bipolar disorder, attention deficit disorder, oppositional defiant disorder, and conduct disorders. Van der Kolk described the cycle that occurs with children placed in foster care who are unable to bond securely to any caregiver or to receive genuine love or affection on any ongoing basis.

Many individuals with ID were moved around among multiple placements as children. According to Van der Kolk (2010), the lack of stability and the resulting lack of opportunity to establish stable attachments becomes its own unique form of trauma. Although Van der Kolk wrote primarily about children from the general population, his research and insights are relevant for individuals with ID. Even individuals with ID who grow up in stable families are still exposed to countless little *t* traumas in the way society treats them, beginning in elementary school. The experience of repeatedly being called the R word is, itself, a trauma experience. If we recognize the many levels of trauma in the lives of individuals with ID, diagnoses might be changed from psychotic disorder NOS (not otherwise specified) or impulse control disorder to developmental trauma disorder, and behavioral problems might finally be seen as actual symptoms of the latter.

References

Barrett, M. J. (2010, March–April). Therapy in the danger zone. *Psychotherapy Networkers*. Available at http://psych.therapynetworker.org

Herman, J. (1997). *Trauma and recovery*. New York: Basic Books.

elopmentally handicapped: The assess-
Psychiatric Aspects of Mental Retardation

Atlanta: Bard Press.

reprocessing (EDMR): Basic principles,

uide to mindsight and neural integration.

L. W. (Eds.). (2007). *Traumatic stress: and society*. New York: Guilford Press.

Trauma.

7

Stabilization

If we continue with the assumption that 90% of behavioral issues are emotion based, stemming from both large T and small t trauma and associated responses, the next course of action would then be to look at how people dealing with the effects of trauma, possibly with the true diagnosis of developmental trauma disorder, can be supported so that they can truly stabilize and enjoy their lives. The effects of trauma identified by Judith Herman (1997)—lack of sense of safety, disconnection, and powerlessness—are logical starting points for examining stabilization and prevention. In the ID field, we have long been reactive when it comes to behavioral issues. We write and implement behavior management and behavior support plans only when behavioral problems occur.

An individual once shared with me that he liked to have a behavior problem periodically. "Why?" I asked him. "Because that way I can have a behavior plan and get rewards. If you are too good, no one gives you anything." I thought this was very insightful. Prevention makes so much more sense than reactive management of behavioral issues. Allowing people to learn about their own happiness and to learn to access positive resources themselves makes so much more sense than fostering dependence on rewards for good behaviors.

Even more importantly, without a sense of safety individuals have a very difficult time making any behavioral or emotional progress. No one is able to thrive when they are feeling threatened. The operative word is "feeling." Staff may assert that individuals with ID are quite safe, even though they claim to feel unsafe with a particular co-resident, co-worker or staff. The perception of a lack of safety is psychologically the same as being unsafe (Herman, 1997). I believe it is important that we focus on the creation of a sense of safety as part of the foundation needed in the recovery from the effects of trauma and the ability to thrive.

Sense of Safety

Safety for a person with an intellectual disability can mean a lot of things. It can mean being physically safe and not being around unpredictable people who may become volatile. This may seem like a small issue, but, in fact, many staff who work with individuals with ID have their own trauma issues. Many are just a step away from needing a great deal of assistance themselves. In many states, direct care workers serving individuals with ID are very low paid. Employees with higher levels of education, skill, and/or work experience often do not choose this type of work.

To illustrate, let's return to the example of Trudy from the last chapter. At Trudy's home, one of the staff members was allowing her abusive husband to visit her at work and engage in altercations while she was on the job. Trudy felt unsafe. One agency that I worked at was very proud of its policy of considering convicted criminals for jobs and of giving those hired a second chance. This was a wonderful policy, but unfortunately, some of these ex-criminals had committed violent crimes and had anger management issues behind closed doors. Some of them were also very open about their past offenses with the individuals with ID with whom they were working. Understandably, these individuals did not feel safe. I would work with people very intensely, but they would never stabilize. My staff and I did therapy, trained staff, wrote many plans, and worked hard to help these individuals stabilize, but we repeatedly had negative results. One day I read the mission statement of the organization, which I had passed in the hallway for many months without ever really seeing. The mission statement did not talk about serving individuals with disabilities. Instead, it talked about providing employment opportunities for people with criminal histories.

From that point forward, before beginning work, I learned to read the mission statement of every agency that hired me. I understood why people were having behavioral issue after behavioral issue. I began asking people how they felt in their homes. Many were concerned about not upsetting staff; sometimes aggression or property destruction occurred more out of fear and mounting anxiety than out of anger. I understood why all of our anger management groups had not helped. These folks were anxious in their own homes. Many had come from abusive backgrounds and were triggered by conflicts, loud voices, or the use of certain offensive words. The behaviors that we saw were often trauma responses, a mixture of triggered implicit memories and anxieties associated with fears based on past difficulties. It was unlikely that we could have stabilized anyone in such an environment.

Sometimes people do not feel safe with their housemates. Although individuals with ID are often told that they can choose where they live, the reality is that in community-based agencies, the residential situation is based on openings, not choices. The administrators are doing the choosing. This may make for some uncomfortable or downright threatening situations. If Joey has a housemate who periodically becomes upset, throws objects, and sometimes even attacks Joey, Joey will never feel safe.

The same situation may occur in a work or classroom setting. If there is an individual with difficulties, perhaps his or her own trauma-based responses, those around this individual are often on edge, particularly if they have been attacked in the past. The instructors or job coaches may tell the others to just ignore the person with the difficulties or not to worry because the person has a behavior management plan. But if we had a co-worker who periodically attacked others physically, we could rest assured that we would soon be able to say goodbye to that person. Or we may not have a chance because the police may be too quickly carting that person away. Not so when you have ID. Volatile people with such issues often comprise your work group. Life is never safe. Being retraumatized is almost a way of life.

Emotional Safety

Several years ago, I was consulting with a group of trained therapists in an outpatient clinic serving individuals with ID. They requested training on conducting therapy with people with ID. After several training sessions, we did case reviews. A particulary poignant one was the case of Bob. When behavioral issues are focused on out of context, even if it is done therapeutically, we often miss the true cause of the difficulty. If someone is in an emotionally difficult or unsafe situation, he or she cannot progress to the next level until that situation changes, regardless of therapeutic supports.

Bob

Bob and Ken had resided in the same local institution together for over 10 years but were now living in a community-based residence. Like many individuals in institutional settings, they had had a homosexual relationship, but Bob was truly in love with Ken. Once they moved into the community, Ken became very excited at the prospect that he could now have a girlfriend. He met a woman named Jenny, and they began seeing each other. After many months, the relationship became serious, and Jenny began to spend the night at Ken and Bob's house once or twice a month. Bob became highly agitated in response.

The therapist had tried many approaches to help Bob learn relaxation and anger management skills. All of his efforts seemed to be having no effect. In reviewing the case, I asked the therapist how he would feel if his wife broke up with him, continued to live with him in their home, and once or twice a month had her new boyfriend there to spend the night. The therapist acknowledged that this would be absolutely horrible. I then pointed out that this was the situation that Bob was basically in. No one had asked Bob whether he minded watching his ex engage in a new relationship in his very own home. Bob, like any of us would, did not feel emotionally safe in his home. Every night Bob's feelings of hurt, abandonment, and rejection were triggered as he listened to Kenny talk to Jenny on the phone. These feelings culminated during Jenny's visits. Worse, Bob had experienced a lot of loss and rejection throughout his life: His family had left him in the institution years ago and not returned to visit. With Kenny, Bob experienced rejection and abandonment again.

The concept of emotional safety considers the degree to which the individual feels safe. It cannot be measured objectively, and yet a self-report tells all. Bob's story shows just how important it is to ask individuals whether they are comfortable in their homes, whether anything or anyone causes them discomfort or fear, or whether there is anything that they would like to change.

Betty

Betty was a lovely woman who had lived her entire life in the city. She was moved by her agency into a home in the suburbs, with two other individuals. The agency assumed that she would love her new home. Instead, she became convinced that there were demons in the woods behind her. She heard animal sounds at night, possibly owls, foxes, and deer, and concluded that they were demons. In addition to an intellectual disability, Betty had had to cope with mental illness throughout her adult life. At her new suburban home, she could not be convinced that there were no demons in the woods, and this conviction would keep her awake at night screaming, causing staff and her other housemates to complain bitterly. Staff took Betty to the psychiatrist to get her medication increased. In the psychiatrist's assessment, Betty was having delusions. But actually, never having previously heard animals at night, Betty's interpretation very accurately fit her worldview. Not only had she never encountered such noises, she had also had a very religious upbringing in which she had been taught a great deal about demons. She had never before identified exactly what the reverends had been talking about, but now everything had come together for Betty, and she was convinced that she knew what demons sounded like. Moving Betty, rather than increasing her medication, would have been the appropriate solution to this problem. When Betty finally did move, due to a physical problem, she calmed down considerably. She finally felt safe.

Empowerment

Those of us who have worked in the field between the late 1980s and the 2000s have heard the term "empowerment" bandied about in regards to individuals with disabilities. We have seen self-advocacy movements that were very exciting but not as far-reaching as one might have hoped. We have seen self-determination and essential life planning (Smull 1996) gain currency as wonderful approaches to individual choice. However, we have all seen that in community-based living programs, choice is not always what it appears to be.

Real Choice Versus Fake Choice

I have sat at many wonderful annual reviews for individuals with ID in which each individual was given the opportunity to make choices about his or her life and set great goals pertaining to these choices. I have then returned a year later for the next annual review, at which more wonderful choices were made and more great goals were set. However, the only real change that could distinguish the first meeting from the next was the date on the individual plan and behavior plan. Despite all the choices presented and selected, the plans written, the goals set, and the dreams discussed, it was very likely that a year later, the individual would still be living with the same people, still working in the same setting, and still having the same issues with staff and peers.

I have known people who have said every year for many years that they wanted to live with their significant other. Every year they are told to continue working on their behavior so that they can earn this privilege. If this were the case for all of us, none of us would ever be married. This approach might solve the problem of divorce, but there would be countless lonely people in the world. Why is it that people with ID have to jump through so many hoops to be allowed the privilege of marriage, whereas the rest of us, with all of our imperfections, can live together, marry, hook up, or pursue whatever other arrangement we wish to choose at any given time?

This is a lack of power. Without real choices, we cannot learn, grow, explore, discover and find out who we really are and what we really want in this life. We are very skilled in providing fake choices to individuals with ID: They believe, at the time, that they are making a choice and being supported, but months later, their situation still has not changed.

Herman (1997) described victims of trauma as feeling powerless and paralyzed in their situations; thus, the abused wife does not leave her bad marriage, the rape victim does not date, and the person who is a victim of violent crime no longer ventures out. The act of abuse robs a person of a sense of personal power. A very important part of the healing process is regaining power over one's own life. If you have ID and you are bearing the emotional burden of past trauma, it is very unlikely that you will be able to heal totally without having power over your life.

Choice is power. Until we transition, as a field, from offering individuals fake choices to offering them real ones, we cannot expect people to heal from past trauma and to change their behavioral patterns. Frequently unable to express their frustration, individuals with ID often manifest these feelings in behavioral difficulties. In the case of fake choice, they know that they were given a choice, they know that all the right things were said, but somehow change did not come about. Instead of being able to identify the fakeness of the choice, they often become frustrated: mad with themselves, mad with the world, and unable to understand that this is because the choices they were given were not real. Those emotions build and manifest behaviorally. The individual is blamed and told, "see, that's why you can't have [X]," X being whatever the fake choice falsely promised: a new job, marriage, or a new place to live. A vicious cycle ensues.

The behaviorist comes in and says that the behavior is for attention, and attention becomes the issue. Or maybe escape. But the underlying issue, the lack of real choice, is never addressed. We need to facilitate real choices for real people with ID if we are going to help them move past being helpless victims who self-destruct on a regular basis toward becoming truly empowered individuals.

Establishing Connections

In her book *Trauma and Recovery,* Judith Herman wrote:

> The Core Experiences of psychological trauma are disempowerment and discon-
> nection from others. Recovery, therefore, is based upon the empowerment of the
> survivor and the creation of new connections. Recovery can take place only within
> the context of relationships, it cannot occur in isolation. (Herman, 1997, p. 133)

The very condition of having an ID is a condition of alienation. Those with ID are excluded from so many activities in the mainstream of human life. Exclusion may begin at a young age, with placement in special education classes, and continue through adolescence and into adulthood, as individuals with ID are often unable to earn a driver's license, get a part-time job in the community while going to school, or enter college. Some do penetrate these barriers, but most do not and they often feel the sting of exclusion.

In addition to this, Herman (1997) pointed out that those suffering with PTSD are often disconnected from the world around them. In the worst case scenarios, they are also disconnected from themselves, thus developing a variety of dissociative disorders in response to trauma and through disconnection from self and others.

We do not see many examples of multiple personality disorders among individu-als with ID, but we do see examples of dissociative disorders. I have had individuals describe to me that they do not feel as though they are in their skin. Others have told me that they have another name and insist that they are a different person, though not multiple people. One woman who was repeatedly sexually abused by her father while growing up adopted another name and another identity when she came to live with a community agency. It wasn't until her records came that the agency knew she had a completely different name. It takes a great deal of time and patience to establish a connection with individuals who have been alienated and disconnected both from themselves and from society, but it is a tremendously worthwhile endeavor and often the key to eliminating behavioral problems.

Attachment Disorder

Mary Ainsworth (1973) built upon the work of developmental psychologist John Bowlby and studied the attachment and bond between infants and their mothers or primary caregivers. She identified the relationship of the infant to the primary caregiver as that infant's template for all future relationships. She looked, in particular, at attachments that were not consistent, or up and down in the level of sensitivity of the caregiver to the needs of the child, and at attachments that were never secured. The children, as they grew, developed patterns of insecurity when the attachment was not consistent and patterns of avoidance when it was weak or nonexistent. In other words, early childhood experience helped to form the degree to which the individual could trust and bond with others in the world.

Individuals with ID born in unstable situations, such as to a mother addicted to crack cocaine or chronic alcohol consumption, are unlikely to form secure bonds with their mothers. Children with prenatal cocaine exposure or fetal alcohol syndrome, therefore, are likely to have difficulties bonding with and trusting others in the future, due to the difficulties that their mothers had in the child's first year of life. In addition, some mothers who have infants with genetic disorders go through a period of mourning in which they withdraw from them. Thus, the child's bond with and ability to trust others is hampered by that early experience.

Now add trauma experience to these attachment issues. The combination is an unstable home and a child with ID. This is the recipe for an individual who cannot make strong connections with others and has difficulty trusting. These attachment issues can take many forms: for example, adults who are overly attention seeking and never satisfied may even manufacture crises in order to gain attention if the attachment has been insecure. Other times, when the attachment has been almost nonexistent, adults become avoidant and trust no one.

These issues pertaining to attachment create problems in the connections that individuals form as adults. According to some, they affect every aspect of the adult lifestyle. Peluso, Peluso, Buckner, Kern, and Curlette (2009) demonstrated that patterns of attachment established in the first year of life persist and are even seen in the individual's approach to life and lifestyle throughout adulthood. They call for more research exploring the ways in which people are able to grow past these patterns.

It is very likely that many individuals with ID have both insecure and avoidant attachment disorders. This makes bonding with the individual even more critical since there have been lifelong patterns of either insecurity or mistrust or, in some cases, both. How do we help such individuals? It is important that the staff establish bonds with the individuals and that the individuals be encouraged to establish bonds with each other. A person in isolation does not recover from trauma-based experiences.

Teaching Staff to Establish Connections

Currently in the field of intellectual disability, we teach staff to control, shape, and modify individuals' behaviors. Instead, we can teach staff to create connections with these individuals and assist them in recovering from their difficult and traumatic experiences by offering them safe and healing relationships. We can also teach the staff to assist the individuals in establishing friendships and/or a relationship with a significant other. If we redirect our training efforts toward this skill set, and staff learn to build healthy and meaningful connections with the individuals with whom they work, we will definitely see decreases in behavioral issues. We will see even more decreases in behavioral issues if we teach the staff to facilitate friendships, social relationships, and, when pertinent, romantic relationships among individuals with ID.

How do we do this? First of all, staff should be required to have structured time each day for interaction with the individuals with whom they work—not to work on goals but to listen to them dialogue about life issues. We can train staff in active listening skills. We can also train them in relationship-building skills. I have conducted such trainings for many years and have always found that staff are able to pick up and implement these skills relatively easily when there is an administration that supports and promotes the implementation of these relationship and listening skills.

Second, staff must receive sensitivity training and be made highly aware of how it feels to have an intellectual disability in this world. Staff must be trained to empathize and understand through the use of experiential sensitivity training. I have also conducted such trainings repeatedly and have found that staff with varied educational backgrounds are all able to learn to empathize and understand ID and the trauma associated with having ID in this society. Once staff have acquired that level of empathy, they naturally work very differently with individuals.

Finally, staff can be trained in skills that will help them to assist the individuals they work with to build relationships with peers. Staff can be taught to be a social coach. The coaching model works very well. When staff view their role as a coach, they can foster and support individuals in building social relationships. Within the context of the individual's relationship with the coaching and caring staff and their relationship with peers, the individual can finally move past the effects of past traumas that they may be stuck in and begin to heal.

If psychologists and administrators give staff the message, through training and daily operations, that the way staff help individuals with their behaviors is to connect with them and assist them in connecting with others, then behavioral issues decrease. All of us who work in the field know that individuals behave much differently with staff that they have a positive and close relationship with versus with staff who do not place a priority on interacting with individuals and do not have a close relationship with them. The relationship between staff and the individuals they serve is critical; and the necessary relationship-building skills can be taught to staff. Individuals also have far more meaning and hope in their lives when they have a significant social network (Seligman, 2011).

Staff are not the problem; they reflect the messages we give them. If psychologists convey the message that staff should use techniques to control behaviors, then they become controlling and often engage in power struggles. If administrators convey the message that the priority of a community residential and/or day program is all about money and the bottom line, then staff do not tend to value the individuals with whom they work and may look at their employment solely as a source of income. If administrators and psychologists send the message that staff are changing the lives of individuals who have been through so much by building meaningful relationships with them and by helping them to build peer relationships, then staff will, generally, build relationships. And as Judith Herman (1997) asserts, people heal in the context of relationships, not in isolation.

Therapy

Trauma may be inherent, in this society, to the experiences of those with ID, but to return to the little *t*–big *T* distinction made by Shapiro (2001), it is very important that anyone with an identified big *T* trauma experience receive therapy from a professional therapist. These experiences include sexual abuse of any kind, from rape to molestation; an abrupt or traumatic loss of a loved one; experience of an accident or disaster; abandonment by one's family; removal from one's family; and physical abuse of any kind. The ideal therapist to treat these traumas should have experience working with individuals with ID. It is also important that the therapist include, either in a small portion of each session or in one out of four or five sessions, the staff person who works most closely with the individual.

Having conducted therapy in many different ways with individuals with ID, I recommend that in a clinic setting, the staff be partially involved. That way, any issues that the individual may be having can be brought to light, conflicts with staff or issues in the home can be discussed with staff present, and the therapist can assist the individual with ID in self-advocacy and conflict resolution. With individuals with ID, it is important not to work as a therapist in a vacuum. It is helpful to engage the staff and assist the individual in communicating with the staff but only for a portion of the session. It is also important that the individual have his or her own one-on-one time with the therapist. The same is true of a family member. Some time in the session with the family member is helpful, but it is very important to have time alone with the individual.

If an agency has referred someone for therapy, it is important that the therapy not be done in isolation but that involved staff or family participate in a portion of the therapy and can assist with follow-through as well. A therapist experienced in working with individuals with ID is, most likely, going to be aware of this necessity. Other therapists may need to be asked to include staff or family for a portion or percentage of sessions. Therapy is critical because the individual must have the treatment on the psychological and emotional level that is needed. This is part of creating a sense of safety, connection, and empowerment. Within the therapeutic relationship, the person with ID who has experienced trauma can get treatment and begin to heal. Staff involvement is critical so that the safety, empowerment, and connections made in the session can be maintained and built upon throughout the rest of the week.

I have worked in a clinic, and I have worked within an agency setting. I admire and appreciate the community-based agencies that are willing to employ psychologists and/or therapists in-house and call on them as resources for resolving behavioral issues, training staff, and counseling both individuals and groups. In my experience, these are the agencies that produce the most long-lasting results in creating safe environments where individuals can heal and become happy.

References

Ainsworth, M. (1973). The development of infant–mother attachment. In B. M. Caldwell & H. N. Ricciuti (Eds.), *Review of child development research* (Vol. 3, pp.1–94). Chicago: University of Chicago Press.

Herman, J. (1997). *Trauma and recovery.* New York: Basic Books.

Peluso, P., Peluso, J., Buckner, J., Kern, R., & Curlette, W. (2009). Measuring lifestyle and attachment: An empirical investigation linking individual psychology and attachment theory. *Journal of Counseling and Development, 87,*

Seligman, M. (2011). *Flourish.* New York: Free Press.

Smull, M. (1996). PDF available at http://www.allenshea.com/brochure.pdf

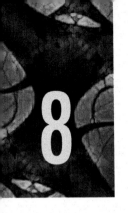

8

Trauma-Informed Crisis Prevention

Assessment

We cannot talk about crisis intervention unless we talk first about prevention. What matters most, actually, is to understand, support, and prevent. We can train staff to focus on prevention rather than train them with a primary focus on crisis intervention. In order to train staff on prevention, we must first look at each individual and understand each person's triggers. Formulas do not work. Crisis prevention has to be based on an individual knowledge of the person with ID.

It is very important to know the backgrounds of the individuals. A thorough social history should be completed and made available to staff. It is important that any known or alleged abuse or neglect be discussed in the history in as much detail as possible. This knowledge should be shared with staff. It is so important that all staff working with the individual understand the level of trauma that that individual has experienced and that all staff be trained in working with people who have experienced trauma.

As has been discussed, everyone's trauma experience is different, and everyone has levels of trauma damage. I believe that professionals should be used to assess the level of trauma and the level of damage rather than to do functional assessments. A functional assessment conducted by a professional will lead others to conclude that the behavior the individual is having is manipulative, being performed as a means to an end. A trauma assessment should indicate the level of trauma damage that has been endured, the amount and frequency of trauma events, triggers of any possible posttraumatic stress response, and what safety looks like for that individual.

A clinical professional should be able to assess the best way to serve that person in order for the person to feel safe and to identify what that individual's unique triggers are. A professional will recognize how merely giving an individual a number of an administrator or access to a manager helps ensure a feeling of safety with staff, comforting the individual with the knowledge that someone will be there to back him or her up if staff become unsafe in any way.

If a trained professional is able to conduct a proper clinical interview, he or she should be able to detect signs and symptoms of trauma. There are also trauma assessment tools that are helpful and can be accessed in a number of ways. I recommend *Acute Stress Disorder,* a handbook edited by Richard Bryant and Alison Harvey (2000), as a wonderful resource for identifying PTSD and assessing the level of trauma and stress an individual is experiencing. Traditional assessments can be modified by a therapist experienced in working with individuals with ID. I highly recommend that such assessments be conducted with individuals who are having behavioral difficulties.

Mental Health Plan

It is important that those events, objects, situations, or people that trigger an individual's trauma response are listed and made known to staff. I propose that a qualified professional write a mental health plan rather than a behavior management plan or even a behavior support plan. Later in the book, I outline a proposed template for a mental health plan. It should, above all, include an assessment of triggers for trauma responses for that individual and identify what that individual requires in order to feel safe.

For example, if John was physically abused by staff in an agency he lived in as a teenager and that abuse occurred after John did not do his chores correctly, staff must be told, via a mental health plan, how to work with John on chore completion in a manner in which he feels appreciated, not threatened, and to request chore completion in a manner that does not trigger a trauma response in John. I have seen staff trigger a trauma response in different individuals on more than one occasion by criticizing a chore that the individual has completed. In other circumstances, such a response might be considered an overreaction. But in individuals with ID, it is important that instead of looking at the staff request that triggered the reaction as an antecedent and then writing a behavior plan for noncompliance, we see past the noncompliance issue into the emotion-based trauma response.

Hypervigilance

Some individuals are also highly sensitive to noise. People who have experienced trauma are often hypervigilant and startle easily, look constantly for signs of trouble or danger, and are unable to relax. This hypervigilance can be seen in many individuals with ID who appear to have generalized anxiety disorders that are purely psychiatric. There is a vigilance or a determined attention to safety due to a need to protect themselves, even when no danger is present. This is commonly seen when there has been trauma (Van der Kolk, McFarlane, & Weisaeth, 1996). Sometimes, individuals who have had experiences with abusive staff are very concerned, even obsessed, with staffing, staff patterns, and the possibility of changes in staff. It is important that we understand their need to be assured of being with safe staff and to be informed about the staffing of their homes. It can be very disturbing to return to one's own home and be greeted by a stranger who tells you what to do. This is not an experience that any of us would want. In the mental health plan, there should be a section on issues of safety and whatever else the individual may be particularly concerned about or, in some cases, hypervigilant about. In this way, specific details can be given about the best approach to introducing new staff and situations to the individual.

Paraprofessional Counseling

Staff can participate in a very rudimentary form of paraprofessional counseling when adequately trained. This training should primarily focus on active listening skills taught by a clinical professional. If we do not train staff in this area, they often revert to the interaction styles with which they were raised. Thus, we have the "house parent" mode and the "good client or bad client" judgments that prove only ineffectual at best and detrimental, even punitive, at worst. We must train staff when they begin work to understand and utilize active listening skills. These skills should include an awareness of body language, purposeful eye contact, and a communication style that involves, in turn, reflecting, paraphrasing, empathizing, encouraging, and probing with open-ended questions. Staff should be taught not to rush to make judgments or to give advice but to use these listening skills before all else, in order to assist individuals in expressing their feelings and releasing their emotions.

Next, staff should be trained in basic problem-solving skills. These skills should include how to identify the problem, generate solutions with the individual, and assist the individual in choosing a course of action. Finally, staff should be trained in follow-up and support of the individual. These are basic skills that do not require a master's degree. The issue is that staff interact all day with individuals without being given training on the proper techniques for listening and problem solving. So instead, staff do whatever comes to mind, which may not always be productive or therapeutic. Administrators and professionals need to take responsibility for ensuring that staff have adequate interactive skills. This can be done through training conducted by professionals. In addition, those professionals must make clear in training what expectations exist about what staff should not be doing: not giving their personal opinions and not engaging in actual therapy, for example. Staff need to be taught to recognize the difference between professional and paraprofessional counseling and when to seek the assistance of professional therapists.

With this training now provided to staff, the mental health plan can incorporate structured listening and dialoguing time each day for the individual who needs support. This might entail an outline of a 20-min period each day during which the individual would be the sole focus of the staff. Perhaps this might occur when the individual arrived home from work or after dinner, depending on the home schedule and the individual's preference. This is essential for individuals who have had any kind of trauma experience in the past. Each day they must feel as though someone is listening to them and someone is concerned about whatever they may be going through.

Listening to individuals each day and assisting them in processing their feelings and working out solutions to their problems is a great act of prevention. Often the behavioral issues that we witness are based on emotions that have been stored up and unexpressed and then triggered. Individuals with ID who have been suffering what Judith Herman (1997) called "complex trauma" are like emotional minefields. They cannot calm themselves when the explosion occurs because the emotion has been building for so long.

If we train staff to listen to individuals in a manner that assists the latter to express their emotions, we help to release the emotion daily and are not as likely to see large explosions due to emotional buildup and trauma triggers. A part of human life and an important aspect of direct care work involves listening to what individuals are feeling. When individuals are not verbal, we must still focus on listening to whatever language they are using. John McGee (1987) in *Gentle Teaching* wrote about understanding people's language and dialoguing with them even though they may not be verbal. It is important to spend at least 20 min each day solely focused on understanding and listening to the individuals with whom we are working. Such consistent acts drastically reduce behavioral incidents.

Psychiatric Visits

Many times I have observed a negative cycle in which staff notice that an individual with ID has been agitated, make an appointment with the psychiatrist without consulting with anyone else, and succeed in getting the individual's medication increased. The individual usually gains more weight as a result of increased medication, becomes lethargic, and, yes, stops exhibiting negative behaviors but also doesn't do much of anything at all. The person is too stoned to do much.

Often, the individual is actually grappling with some emotional issue, and that is why he or she appears agitated or is having behavioral difficulties. The individual may even be experiencing symptoms of PTSD. In either case, the individual might have benefited more from a therapeutic intervention as opposed to a chemical one. The agency administrators and professionals would have made a therapeutic intervention possible if they had been aware that there was an issue. Direct care staff are, in many cases, making clinical decisions and providing the psychiatrists with the information that prompts medication increases without having the necessary background for such decisions.

It is important, when dealing with issues of prevention, that staff be trained to work together with the rest of the individual's team to provide information to the psychiatrist. This information should include records on sleep patterns, eating patterns, gain or loss of interest in specific activities, hygiene, amount of verbalizations and dialogue, and work or daytime performance. It may be the case that staff are having a personality clash with the individual and report it as the individual's agitation. Psychiatric problems do exist; but part of prevention is to train direct care staff to provide to psychiatrists proper data and any other information needed to make an informed decision on how to medicate the individual correctly.

This is no small concern. Someone on the wrong medication can have serious behavioral problems and exhibit a great deal of agitation. Someone on too much medication or inappropriate medication can also be put at serious medical risk. Proper psychiatric practice requires correct information from the direct care staff and from team members. The psychiatrist cannot operate in a vacuum; this information is critical. It must be accurate and appropriate in order for the psychiatrist to prescribe effectively.

Earlier in the book, I gave examples of individuals who died as a result, in all likelihood, of lethal medication interactions. It is important that anyone caring for an individual with ID also have a relationship with a pharmacy and pharmacist who is aware of all the medications being prescribed and of possible interaction issues. The mental health plan should outline what information should be reported to the psychiatrist, what the medications are for, and the actual meaning and implications of the individual's psychiatric diagnosis. It is crucial that all direct care staff and managers understand this information.

Communication

Carr et al. (1997) asserted that communication is the key in behavioral issues with individuals with ID. They illustrated their argument with many examples of individuals who had behavioral problems until communication was increased between the individuals and the direct care staff working with them. Time and again, as staff increased communication and improved rapport, problem behaviors in the individuals with whom they worked radically decreased. In situations where individuals are not highly verbal, it is particularly important that staff find other ways to communicate. Herman (1997) wrote about the importance of connecting with others in order to heal from trauma. Carr et al. wrote something very similar: Communication increases the connection, and the "rapport" that is built between individuals and staff is that very connection that facilitates the healing process.

Cookie

One woman who resided in an agency that I worked in had a small biting problem. She would bite others when she became anxious or upset. She took a few lunges at me on two separate occasions. When I first came to this agency, she had been having severe biting, hitting, and kicking problems. Then she miraculously calmed down. What was the key? A gifted staff person, whom we will call Angie. What did Angie do? Cookie was minimally verbal and talked very little, could just barely say her own name—or so we thought. Staff in the past had barked orders at her, and although she understood, she would not respond in words. Angie began talking to her and listening as though Cookie were talking back. She started telling Cookie how much she loved Cookie. Pretty soon Cookie started responding and saying " I love you" in return to Angie. Cookie began to kiss instead of trying to bite. I watched Cookie transform into a loving person when she was with Angie. She began talking in one-word sentences, trying very hard to communicate with Angie. Angie talked and listened and talked and talked with Cookie.

Then one day, unfortunately, Angie had some trouble with the law. I never did find out what it was, but she had to leave her position for a "hiatus." Cookie quickly regressed. I visited her in her home. There I observed a staff member speaking in a demanding and demeaning manner toward Cookie and complaining bitterly, while Cookie was in the room, about having to work with her. Cookie soon began to make attempts to bite that staff person, and even though we tried desperately to get this employee to talk differently to Cookie, the damage was done. Cookie's behavior problems returned.

At Cookie's day program, we were able to teach the staff to talk to her kindly and to use words of caring and love. Cookie settled back down at the day program and stopped biting there, although she continued at home. Communication, particularly kind and caring communication, as Angie had shown us, was the best treatment for Cookie.

Safety

As with stabilization, safety is a key factor in prevention. Many individuals with ID have come to believe that the best defense is a good offense. When they perceive themselves not to be safe, they will lash out so that others will not attack first. I have witnessed this occurrence on many occasions. It can often be seen when an individual is in a new situation or a situation in which that person feels threatened. When individuals transfer programs or sites, it is important to have gradual transitions in which familiar people are involved.

Individuals also do not feel safe in situations where they have experienced abuse or neglect in the past. If individuals have been in an institution where they have experienced abuse and they are left in the same setting, it is very likely that they will exhibit behavioral problems as long as they remain in that setting. They should be placed elsewhere and given a sense of support during such a change. When Maryland closed the institution Rosewood recently, 15 individuals came to the agency Emerge for community-based services. Of those individuals, 12 had significant behavioral problems when they arrived in the agency, with behavioral events occurring, in every case, at least monthly and in some cases weekly. Every single individual has since experienced a significant decline in behavioral difficulties. Not one person has had monthly events, and there has been at least a 60% decline in episodes for each one of the 12 individuals. Why? Because they are no longer living in settings in which abuse is alleged to have occurred. Each of them is now living with no more than two other people in a home setting, not with over 20 in an institutional setting in which they were vulnerable to attacks from other individuals and vulnerable to staff who were not closely supervised and did not follow correct procedures. Other agencies in the Maryland area have had the same result. Over and over, stories have been recounted of individuals who had daunting behavioral "reputations" acquired during their years living in the institution but who, when placed in the community, no longer displayed those same behavioral patterns. And when behavioral issues did occur, they were much less intense in both degree and duration.

The experience of feeling safe has had a profound effect on each person who transitioned from the institution. They have been supported by the staff and supported by the management and administration of these community agencies. They have been made aware of the checks and balances in place to secure their safety on a daily basis. It has made a tremendous difference.

Connection

As discussed in Chapter 7, connection to others is crucial in the ability to heal from trauma. The connection needed to prevent behavioral problems has been explored in three different contexts: therapy; paraprofessional counseling and active listening on the part of direct care staff; and communication with an individual who is kind and caring in nature and ensures the connection.

Empowerment

Prevention is no more than common sense: Avoid power struggles. Sometimes staff may be overly rigid with a house rule, protocol, or restriction in a manner in which a multitude of problems are created as a result. It is best to remember that individuals with ID have rights, including the right to make mistakes from time to time. If staff assume a parental role, then it is likely that staff will find themselves engaging in parent–child power struggles. It is best to assist staff in assuming the coaching model and coach people through their strengths and weaknesses to make the best decisions for themselves.

Herman (1997) pointed out that people who have experienced trauma often feel as though they are powerless. Those feelings of powerlessness can set the stage for further trauma responses. People with ID, because of their frequent histories of trauma, can be triggered even more by feeling powerless or by the perception that they do not have power over their lives. This perception is likely to occur in the midst of a power struggle. Their trauma response can appear behavioral but actually be due to a panicked reaction to the loss of personal power or to the perceived loss of that power.

Positive Identity Development

In a previous book (Harvey, 2009), I discussed the importance of assisting individuals with ID in developing a positive sense of who they are. The book is primarily for clinicians, but the concept applies to anyone working with individuals with ID. We often act based on our own view of ourselves. If we are seen as troublemakers, we might actually throw ourselves into creating trouble. Many of us changed our behaviors when we became professionals: We started dressing differently, tidied up our language, got more organized, and so on. Those of us who are parents may also have changed when we transitioned into that role: We no longer took unnecessary risks, we maybe kept all of our activities completely legal, and, in general, we acted more responsibly. Those are examples of behavior changing as a result of a change in sense of identity.

Individuals with ID can make profound, self-motivated changes in their behaviors as a result of changes in their sense of identity. When they are people with outside or community jobs, they may change the ways in which they act during the day. For example, they may choose to resolve conflicts differently, through their role at work, and consciously avoid physical and/or verbal altercations. They may change their social behavior after becoming a girlfriend or boyfriend and speak more nicely, make better eye contact, even exercise better hygiene choices. These positive changes in roles should be supported and encouraged by staff. A positive sense of identity in the world is an essential to the building of a meaningful life. It is also an effective method of behavioral change. Change that comes from within is much more likely to last than change imposed from the outside—as anyone who has been on a diet mandated by a doctor can likely attest. Change from within is based on seeing oneself differently. That is a view that lasts.

Prevention

In summation, it is so important that administrators, psychologists, and trainers convey to staff working directly with individuals with ID the message that prevention, not crisis management, is the mode of operation. If the staff are trained to prevent incidents, incidents are prevented more often than not. If the staff are trained to focus on crisis intervention, crises occur. This has been my experience. Many agencies become focused on crises without even realizing it. Staff are repeatedly trained in crisis intervention, and prevention is a mere afterthought.

We should use a new approach to behavioral difficulties that is focused on prevention. A mental health plan would gear the staff toward working with the individual on fostering mental health. In contrast, a behavior management plan, even a behavior support plan, focuses the staff and the individual excessively on problem behaviors. This focus is, itself, the problem. A focus on mental health, including stabilization, happiness, and prevention will undoubtedly reduce the occurrence of crises.

References

Bryant, R. A., & Harvey, A. G. (Eds.). (2000). *Acute stress disorder: A handbook of theory, assessment, and treatment.* Washington, DC: American Psychological Association.

Carr, E. G., Levin, L., McConnachie, G., Carlson, J., Kemp, D., & Smith, C. (1997). *Communication-based intervention for problem behavior: A user's guide for producing positive change.* Baltimore, MD: Paul H. Brookes.

Harvey, K. (2009). *Positive identity: An alternative treatment approach for individuals with mild and moderate intellectual disabilities.* Kingston, NY: NADD Press.

Herman, J. (1997). *Trauma and recovery.* New York: Basic Books.

McGee, J. (1987). *Gentle teaching: A nonaversive approach for helping persons with mental retardation.* New York: Human Sciences Press.

Van der Kolk, B. , McFarlane, A., & Weisaeth, L. (Eds.). (1996). *Traumatic stress: The effects of overwhelming experience on mind, body, and society.* New York: Guilford Press.

Trauma-Informed
Crisis Intervention

Trauma-based responses occur when the individual is thrown into fight-or-flight mode either through the perception of danger or some form of threat or through a trigger event that brings up the emotions stored from a previous traumatic event. In this fight-or-flight mode, or activation of the limbic system, the higher cognitive systems, such as executive functioning, where rational decision making and impulse control monitoring occur, shut down. The individual is not thinking rationally. The task at hand is to assist the individual out of fight or flight and back into rational mode (Siegel, 2010).

This is not done effectively through physical restraint. Many individuals, particularly those who have been physically abused, are retraumatized through physical restraint (Dressler, 2007). The trauma of being physically restrained, no matter how well-meaning the person doing the restraining might be, can actually cause individuals to feel much more threatened and in far more danger than when the behavioral incident first began. They then fight harder and focus more on attempting to free themselves than on calming down. After they have totally given up, they may calm down externally but then have the emotional damage of being held against their will and feeling powerless. The compounded trauma causes further damage.

Complex Posttraumatic Stress Disorder

Herman (1997) proposed the diagnosis of "complex posttraumatic stress disorder" to describe "the syndrome that follows upon prolonged, repeated trauma" (p. 119). It is very likely that individuals who have suffered abuse will respond to that abuse by operating in fight-or-flight mode when feeling threatened and then, having been repeatedly restrained as a result, experience complex PTSD. The complex trauma is caused by the repeated trauma of the act of being physically restrained. The people doing the restraining are often much bigger than the individual and, certainly by virtue of their role as staff, more powerful than the individual. The individual is, therefore, rendered totally powerless and at the mercy of the restrainer. This itself is traumatic.

Individuals who have been in institutions for years and who have the type of brain damage that involves difficulties with impulse control often find themselves repeatedly restrained. I worked with one such individual who had both an intellectual disability and frontal lobe damage. He had come to the agency that I was working with after being in an institution for many years and undergoing countless restraints.

Mark

Mark came to the day program where I worked as a therapist; the program was designed specifically for individuals with a dual diagnosis of ID and mental health issues. Mark had been at the program for only a week, and I had only had one initial session with him. He continued to reside at the local institution for people with ID while attending our program. The state evaluators had felt that he was too "dangerous" to place in the community residentially. In my one session with him, he had begun to tell me about his attachment to his grandmother and how her death, several months ago, had affected him.

I walked in that day, to one of the classrooms, to find Mark holding a table over his head and spewing racial slurs toward a well-meaning staff person. Evidently, that staff person had told Mark how no one gets away with anything and how they will be restrained if necessary. Then the person started to ask Mark about his family. This was just too much for Mark. He was feeling threatened by the staff's verbal show of force, which reminded him of the recent emotional trauma of his grandmother's death. Mark was holding the table up as if readying himself for a major fight. Making sympathetic sounds, I walked up to him.

"Outta the way!" He growled at me.

"What's really bothering you, honey?" I asked with deliberate empathy. "Are you missing your grandmother?"

At that point, he burst into tears and started sobbing.

"The staff don't know about everything you've been through," I continued. "Mark lost his grandmother and seems to be really missing her," I told staff with Mark listening.

Mark put the table down.

"You poor guy, why don't you tell your staff what you've been going through?" I said. With that Mark started telling the staff person about his grandmother's passing. The staff and I listened for a long time. After that, our crisis intervention line was always: "What's really bothering you?"

That line always seems to defuse people. It enables them to check in with the emotion beneath the rage, which is often fear, anxiety, or sorrow. Sometimes there is actual frustration over a problem in which the individual has lost hope; when we ask that question, they might spill out the problem, and then we can quickly engage in problem solving with them as they de-escalate. Most important, that question will cause them to stop and think, thus activating a higher cognitive level than the fight-or-flight limbic system. There is no threat in the question, only concern, and it does cause the individual to have to stop and think, thus switching modes.

To return to Herman's (1997) model, the three factors we want to achieve in crisis intervention are the same factors we need to ensure in stabilization and prevention: safety, connection, and empowerment. The individual must feel safe in order to fully move out of flight-or-fight mode. This might entail removing the individual from the area in which the conflict had begun or removing others from the area, whatever is easiest. The person must connect with someone positively. There has to be someone present who is comforting or someone who already has a good connection with the individual. This connection will help the individual to activate the parasympathetic nervous system and recover his calm more quickly. Finally, there must be a recovery of some sense of personal power. This is possible by assisting the person in solving the problem that might be upsetting him or her or by giving the individual a simple choice. Lack of choice is another form of powerlessness.

Deflation

The best word for crisis intervention is *deflation*. How can the hot air be released? How can the person and the situation be calmed without staff having to restrain or control the individual? Staff need to play the role of the calming coach, rather than that of a controlling force. These ten tips for staff incorporate the three factors of safety, connection, and empowerment in a practical manner and help staff to avoid physical intervention:

1. Lower your voice and show concern on your face.
2. Ask with kindness in your voice, "what is *really* wrong?"
3. Softly coax the person out of the area or away from the target of the anger with suggestions, such as "let's walk" or "tell me exactly what happened."
4. Do not show any fear or anger, no matter what. The person responding must act like the individual who is about to explode is acting in a completely normal manner. When we panic, the upset individual feels even more out of control.
5. Make sure that the staff person or other individual whom that person feels safest with and closest to is at hand or on their way and reassure the person that that person will soon be available to talk to.
6. If there is a specific problem, give the person hope by helping to generate a solution: "We can get some cigarettes soon. How about if we ask the manager to call your house staff to bring some," or whatever brings hope of a solution. Be sure to incorporate some choices so the individual can make a choice in the process. For example: "we can call now and get the house manager to come, or

we can ask [the staff person] Linda if she can lend you a cigarette and you can pay her back tomorrow."

7. Assist the person in coming up with a plan for making the point he or she wanted to make physically by doing so in another way. In one program where I worked, the individuals were particularly oppressed by staff and often became physically aggressive toward staff as a result. In that program, I instituted a write-up form in which the individuals with ID could "write up" the staff. These individuals were empowered to report their staff; they could come to the clinical offices or the administrative office and write up their staff. Reports only went to me (unfortunately), but the individuals felt that they finally had a voice, and aggression against staff decreased considerably. So, in the middle of an escalating incident, I was able to deflate someone, even over the phone, by encouraging him or her to write up the staff when they came to my office the next day.

8. Ground the person in the current reality. Some folks are having such a trauma response that they cannot see that they are safe and in the present. It is important to reiterate to individuals that they are okay, everything is okay, they are with you, and everything is fine as long as they can walk away with you from the situation. People need reassurance to be back in the present. When they have been triggered and they have PTSD, they are flooded with emotions from the past. They need to be reassured that everything is okay, that they are in the present with you, safe and away from the past.

9. They should be congratulated on what they did not do. I have found this technique to be very effective. When one fellow who had a history of physical aggression got upset and threw something, I congratulated him on not hitting anyone and pointed out how far he had come. This completely deflated his anger, and he started to feel good about his small accomplishment, despite himself! I have praised and congratulated many people on their accomplishments of not repeating certain behavioral patterns, even when they are clearly having a hard time. This praise is a fantastic deflator. Many times an individual will agree with me and share how he or she wanted to do more damage or to hurt someone and actually held back. If I had focused only on their negative actions, I would have missed this positive factor and only succeeded in assisting them to escalate further, rather than to de-escalate.

10. Finally, refocus the person on their mission or sense of purpose. It is important to remind individuals that they have a role or mission. I have calmed people down by reminding them that they are a role model for certain others in the program who look up to them, or that their mother or father is counting on them to come home for the weekend, or that they are supposed to be going to help someone later on that day and need to stay calm and focused so they can do what is needed at that crucial time.

These are some techniques that my colleagues and I have used. There are many more, but the crucial component is to stay calm, be positive and supportive, and give the individual hope. These are the critical elements of deflation.

Psychosis

It is important to make the distinction between emotional behavioral events and psychotic episodes. When individuals are actively psychotic, these techniques are almost always ineffective. If they are having a hallucination and are in the midst of a full-blown psychotic episode, they truly need to get immediate emergency services. They can still be helped to calm down, but the chances are that the psychosis will quickly flare back up and they will continue to be in crisis mode. This may occur with individuals who have schizophrenia or schizoaffective disorders. When individuals are actively hallucinating, they are seeing or hearing stimuli that are not accessible to the rest of us but are more real to them than we are. I have been in this situation many times, and no one should debate the reality of the hallucination with the person. That person should be made to feel safe and should be safely delivered to an ER, where, we would hope, admission can occur.

It is important to train staff in the signs that occur when individuals are having a hallucination: They may clearly look at empty spaces, listen, and respond as though someone is present. They may point or talk wildly at themselves. They might even be convinced that someone present is actually a different person. There is no convincing them otherwise, so staff should merely aim to help them feel safe and seek an emergency-level intervention.

Plan

In general, it is important for staff to be informed and trained on each individual's triggers. What events upset that person? Are there any anniversaries of deaths or other losses that act as time triggers? Are holidays difficult? This information should be gathered and made available to staff. In the same vein, staff should know what the person is calmed by. Does he have a comforting hobby? Is there a person that he feels safest with? Or is there a place that the person needs to go to periodically in order to regain calm? This is the kind of information that should be available to staff and that will help with crisis intervention.

I propose a mental health plan that covers all of these items and those factors that help the individual to remain stable and to prevent crises. Rather than a behavioral plan that focuses merely on the actions of the person, which is almost always written after the fact, it is much better to have a plan that looks at assisting the individual in creating and maintaining mental health first and then guides staff through any last-resort interventions. The wellness model has been very effective in the medical field and could certainly be of relevance in the field of individuals with ID who have mental health issues as well.

Eliminating Restraints

There are a number of reasons to eliminate restraints. For one, the risk of retraumatization is high. People who have been physically abused and traumatized as a result are unlikely to see the restraint as a necessary way in which responsible staff assist them in calming themselves. Instead, it is likely that they will lose trust in the staff restraining them and feel fear and other emotions associated with past physical abuse. That staff will have a very difficult time reestablishing the lost trust.

Even more important, however, are the number of deaths that have been caused by restraints. One young man, known to many for his charm and personality, lived several years ago in a Maryland institution. Tragically, he died prematurely at age 30 because he refused to go to the gym at a Maryland institution that served individuals with ID. He was, in fact, killed. The staff person did not like the fact that this individual refused to follow directions, and so the power struggle escalated, culminating in a restraint on a desk that began face up. As was procedure, the staff member called for help. Other staff quickly gathered to assist with the restraint. They quickly moved the man onto the floor. After 3 min, one staff person noticed that the young man had stopped breathing. CPR was started, but it was too late. This young man died as a result of complications due to a physical restraint. More than 20 bruises, contusions, lacerations, and hemorrhages were found on his body. This was clearly not the first time he had been restrained. This tragic death occurred on December 21, 2001.

About 10 years ago, another young man at a Maryland facility refused to follow the staff's directive to go outside. He wanted to remain indoors. An hour later, the young man was dead. He died because the staff member with whom he was arguing chose to restrain him, rather than use any deflation, de-escalation or problem-solving techniques. The staff member used a floor restraint. As happens more than most would like to acknowledge, the restraint was done wrong, and the young man suffocated to death while lying in a prone position (Dressler, 2007). The technical cause of death was prone asphyxia; a number of individuals have died in this manner in the midst of a restraint gone wrong (Luiselli, Bastien, & Putnam, 1998).

Peaceful Practices

It is much easier for staff and for individuals with ID to use peaceful practices. Such practices include clearing the area and letting the person release steam alone, allowing and encouraging the person to leave the area and walk, encouraging the person to "write up" or "report" whomever he or she is upset with, or asking the person what is really wrong and encouraging the person to speak. For those who cannot verbalize their anger or frustration and choose instead to lie down on the floor, it is better if staff sit with them and wait it out rather than trying to drag them somewhere. Eventually they will get up. For self-injurious behaviors, using stimulating items such as massagers and feather dusters and vibrators to stimulate and distract is quite effective. I believe in using community crisis resources for individuals who are truly psychotic and who may also want seriously to hurt themselves or others. With those exceptions, though, peaceful practices can build trust, and staff should be encouraged to use prevention techniques before a situation escalates. Prevention is always easier when restraints are not permitted.

Loving the Hospital

There are those individuals who do love the hospital. Many of them have had earlier trauma, perhaps repeated sexual and physical abuse, and they remember the hospital as the one safe haven in their childhood. These individuals yearn for the hospital during tumultuous times or during times that are triggers for bad memories. During the holidays, many individuals with whom I have worked perform many creative acts in order to get into the hospital. From Thanksgiving until after Christmas many people feel nostalgia for home, wherever that may be. For may individuals with ID who had a childhood filled with traumatic experiences, the safest and best times were in the hospital. Nurses cared for them, food was available, people attended to their needs. Many attempt to get back into the hospital during that period, in order to recapture the sense of safety and belonging.

How do we keep those who love the hospital out of the hospital? If we can provide the emotional supports that are offered during a hospital stay, we can accomplish that goal. First of all, we can ensure that individuals with ID are supported and surrounded by caring and concerned staff. Our folks who love the hospital have certain favorite nurses and aides. It is almost never about the doctors. It is the kind and caring nurse or nurse's aide whom they want to see. Those who seek out psychiatric hospitalizations will talk about groups and the individuals on their floor. Sometimes it is an opportunity for sexual activity. Other times it is free access to food and snacks. I have heard about many perks, but I am always surprised that smokers don't seem to mind giving up smoking as long as they can be in the nurturing hospital setting.

Perhaps we can keep people away from unnecessary hospital stays by employing nurturing and caring staff and providing the individuals we serve with a variety of supportive social opportunities. Many times individuals have told me how they like the staff at hospitals because the staff listen and talk to them. They will also tell me about individuals they have met at the hospital and would like to see again. It appears that the social aspects of hospitalization are both alluring and comforting. These aspects can be re-created within community living settings. Social opportunities and supportive staff can go a long way to help individuals overcome their need for frequent hospitalizations. I have seen this combination work to help people who have been addicted to hospitals wean themselves away from frequent hospitalizations.

Prevention Frame of Mind

The prevention frame of mind within a community agency has to come from the top. The upper management and the executive director or CEO must embrace a mental health approach when serving individuals with ID. This is even more crucial when serving individuals with the dual diagnosis of ID and mental health issues. Rather than making the focus the behavioral problems of the individual, opportunities for socialization and for positive relations with coaching, caring staff should be the focus. A mental wellness model will create a new level of health and enable the organization to move naturally toward prevention and away from crisis intervention. But the message must reach those setting the policies of the agency and those signing the paychecks of the employees. Otherwise, it is easy to slip into crisis mode, in which the focus is on those having behavioral crises and the message is "you get the attention and support you want and need by having crises." Of course, that message, however subtle it may be, is guaranteed to produce crisis-level behavioral issues from many individuals.

Look at the message coming from the top: Is it a reactive crisis response, or is it proactive prevention? The number and nature of incidents will reflect the message. Provide nurturing, support, and socialization consistently, and crisis intervention won't be the dominant mode of operation.

References

Dressler, D. (2007, December). *Current assumptions regarding restraint use.* Paper presented at the Trauma Informed Care Conference, Columbia, MD.

Herman, J. (1997) *Trauma and recovery.* New York: Basic Books.

Luiselli, J. K, Bastien, J. S., & Putnam, R. F. (1998). Behavioral assessment and analysis of mechanical restraint utilization on a psychiatric, child and adolescent inpatient setting. *Behavioral Interventions, 62,* 366–374.

10 Mental Health Plans

The purpose of the mental health plan is to enable the staff to guide the person with whom they are working toward mental health on a daily basis. It is basically a wellness model. If we train the staff to work toward mental health and define what mental health is for each individual, the staff can effectively focus on proactive assistance and foster growth and mental health. If we train the staff to work on controlling behaviors, the staff will be encouraged to engage in power struggles through their well-intentioned efforts toward control of another adult. This is the natural outcome of a control model, in which behaviors are the focus and a functional assessment determining how an individual with ID is manipulating his environment and how he can be outmanipulated by staff, is the guiding principle. We must have a paradigm shift in which the staff are given clear direction to coach the individual with ID toward a new level of mental health. This paradigm shift is from behavioral analysis to positive psychology. Positive psychology is an exciting, growing field based on empirical research that demonstrates principles of human growth and happiness that lead toward higher fulfillment and mental wellness (Snyder & Lopez, 2007). There is no reason why these exciting findings should not be applied to individuals with ID.

I propose that we use a trauma-informed format or plan for individuals with behavioral, traumatic, and mental health difficulties. This plan should include a thorough history, with emphasis on trauma experiences and cause of disability; a list of all possible triggers and difficult anniversaries; an analysis of the individual's happiness on the levels of pleasure, engagement, and meaning; procedures for happiness implementation on all three levels; procedures for prevention of difficulties; procedures for intervention as a last resort; and procedures for recovery to follow any difficult events or incidents. This would provide a blueprint for mental health and be much more thorough than a plan that merely isolates and targets behavioral incidents, without regard for the complete individual. This plan would ideally be designed by an individual with a clinical background. The clinician should thoroughly train the staff in the details of the plan and its implementation.

Recently, I was dialoguing with a group of psychologists in various fields. They observed that older people with Alzheimer's disease, children, and people with ID are always spoken of and quantified by their behaviors. People with normal IQs and status as adults who are functioning in the world may have just as much difficulty with behaviors, but are spoken of in terms of possible mental health problems or, if their status is fairly high, in terms of stress. I was so struck by the observation by my colleague. We tend to use the language of behaviors when people have lower cognitive levels of functionality. In reality they still have the life experience and emotional history of adults, not children. And thus, we need to identify the sources of their behavior as often based on both emotion and past experiences, sometimes traumatic in nature, and disregard in some ways discrepancies in IQ

A mental health plan would guide the individual toward wellness by providing a clear outline for staff that is based on a totally individualized strategy. In this chapter, I will take some of the case histories introduced earlier of different individuals with ID and illustrate how a mental health plan might help staff to assist these individuals in more effective ways.

The Mental Health Plan: A Template

I propose the following outline as a template for the mental health plan:
1. Name
2. Date of birth
3. Location for implementation of plan
4. Plan writer
5. Date
6. Background
7. Trauma experiences
8. Diagnosis
9. Medication
10. Explanation of diagnosis (explain for staff what it really means)
11. Medical issues (explain for staff how these affect lifestyle and mood)
12. Happiness analysis
    a. What that person enjoys for pleasure (provide details)
    b. What activities are most enjoyable for this person for engagement
    c. What brings meaning to this person's life and what meaning is this person seeking
13. Happiness procedure
    a. What staff should do to assist the person to gain pleasure
    b. How staff should support the person in seeking engagement
    c. How staff should assist in fostering relationships and coaching social skills

      d.   What achievements staff should help the person to acknowledge

      e.   How staff should support activities that enhance meaning (such as arranging visits with a beloved grandparent)

14. Trauma response prevention

      a.   List of triggers that are known

      b.   List of known difficult anniversaries

      c.   List of people whom the person is connected to positively

      d.   List of choices that the person should be given consistently

      e.   List of factors required for this individual to feel safe

15. Positive identity development

      a.   Roles that are positive and important to this person

      b.   Ways in which staff need to facilitate the development of self-esteem (including listening procedures)

      c.   Ways in which staff need to facilitate the development of positive peer relations

16. Behavioral incident prevention

      a.   Stressors that the individual has difficulty with and must be prepared for

      b.   How to prepare

      c.   Effective ways to redirect this individual when he or she is having emotional difficulties

      d.   What to do if previous list of triggers occur

      e.   What to do when anniversaries occur

      f.   How to ensure a sense of safety

      g.   How to monitor and report psychiatric issues to the professionals

      h.   Therapeutic interventions required

17. Crisis intervention

      a.   How to emotionally connect with the person when he or she is distressed

      b.   How to remove that person from a difficult situation

      c.   Whom to contact and connect that person with

      d.   How to deal with possible hospitalization (list criteria)

      e.   When to use community emergency services

Example 1

Evelyn

Let's take an example. Evelyn is a young woman with whom I have worked for approximately 8 years. At 36 years old, Evelyn is diagnosed with schizophrenia and moderate mental retardation. She actually can do math quite well and soothes herself by working on math problems. She is more likely to have a borderline IQ, but she tests low as a result of her mental illness and distractibility. Evelyn smokes cigarettes like a car burns gasoline. She is always very concerned about her next cigarette. Evelyn has been on a smoking schedule for many years in order to protect her from running out of cigarettes. When she runs out of cigarettes and cannot get anyone to buy her a pack, she often calls 911. She considers it an emergency.

Evelyn has had a great deal of trauma in her life. She was sexually molested by her stepfather for many years and then raped by a friend of the family when she was a teenager. When she became pregnant as a result, her family forced her to sign papers to give up her baby boy for adoption. When I first met Evelyn, she would talk very loudly about her son and burst into gales of tears. She would scream and cry and ask, "Why did they make me give him up, why, why?" over and over again. She would demand that staff take her to find her son and scream that if they could have their children to raise, why couldn't she have hers?

Evelyn would become very upset around other people's children and ask these questions repeatedly with those children present as well. Evelyn's mother reportedly had her own difficulties with mental illness and would call Evelyn to say that she was coming to visit but then never come. This also made Evelyn very upset.

Evelyn also had problems with promiscuity. She had been known to offer sexual favors for cigarettes. She had been known to date one person and give favors to another for cigarettes or snacks. This promiscuity could be regarded as a behavior problem or seen more deeply as a reflection of Evelyn's lack of self-worth. Evelyn learned early on that her only value in her environment was her ability to be a sexual object. Her actions reflected this.

Several years ago, I was able to help Evelyn to find a wonderful man who adored her. This man has ID and had spent a great deal of his life in an institution because he once set a fire, actually as an adolescent while quite distraught and in an abusive living situation. He was labeled a fire setter from that point on. I would like to note that if someone followed most of us around in our adolescence and wrote reports about us, many of us (myself included), might have had some similar labels. He was not allowed into the community until 3 years ago when he entered the agency where I was working. They have been dating ever since they were introduced and plan to live together. Evelyn no longer trades sexual favors for cigarettes as far as the staff knows.

With all this as an introduction to Evelyn's background, we can now see how our template might be used to prepare a mental health plan for Evelyn that is specific to her history and needs.

MENTAL HEALTH PLAN

NAME: Evelyn Jones

DOB: 9/11/1975

LOCATION: Residential and work settings

PLAN WRITER: Karyn Harvey

DATE: 01/02/2000

BACKGROUND: Evelyn had a very difficult childhood. She was born to Mr. and Mrs. Jones. There is no record of alcohol or drug abuse during the pregnancy. Developmental delays were apparent by age 2, with most major milestones delayed. Language development did not occur until age 3½.

Evelyn's parents were divorced when she was 2 years old, and her mother remarried when Evelyn was 5 years old. Evelyn attended special education classes in a mainstream school. She went all the way through high school, where she received a certificate but no diploma. Evelyn's strength was math and her weakness, reading.

It is reported that Evelyn was sexually molested on a repeated basis by her stepfather. A friend of the family raped Evelyn when she was 15, and she gave birth to a son at age 16. The family secured a closed adoption. Evelyn was placed in an institution for individuals with intellectual disability at age 21. She did not leave the institution until age 28, at which point she entered a community residential agency. She has resided there and attended the day habilitation program since that point.

TRAUMA EXPERIENCES: Evelyn experienced complex trauma in the repeated sexual molestation. She had two major traumatic events: the first was the rape, and the second was the birth and removal of her child. She continues to suffer emotional flashbacks of the removal of her child. She has also had the small trauma of attending special education throughout her schooling in a mainstream school system and the trauma of institutional placement. She does not remember much of her institutionalization and may be blocking traumatic events. She vehemently states that she "hated" institutionalization but cannot provide specific memories.

DIAGNOSIS: Axis I: 295.10 schizophrenia, disorganized type; 309.81 posttraumatic stress disorder; Axis II: 317 mild intellectual disability; Axis III: high blood pressure, high cholesterol; Axis IV: history of sexual abuse, family difficulties; Axis V: Global Assessment of Functioning (GAF): 45.

MEDICATION: Zyprexa, Geodon, Prolixin (see recent physician order forms for doses)

EXPLANATION OF DIAGNOSIS: Evelyn is diagnosed with schizophrenia, of a disorganized type. She has difficulty thinking clearly. She is able to wind herself up into a confused state very easily. She will take a small fact or issue and focus and obsess over it. Next, she will then add delusional thoughts to that fact and spin a complex confused saga that she will believe that she is in the middle of. She feels a sense of frantic panic over any discomfort or deprivation. She may even call 911 because she does not have something she believes that she needs, such as cigarettes or money. She cannot see the separateness of her issues and other people's issues. She becomes upset if people do not feel her concerns are important. Without medication, she is extremely confused and will use nonsensical words and thought systems.

Evelyn is also diagnosed with posttraumatic stress disorder. She had repeated experiences of sexual abuse and a series of traumatic events (see above). Evelyn has, at times, experienced emotional flashbacks. She is easily triggered if she believes that someone is trying to take something from her, and she will have a trauma response that may take the form of aggression or abuse of the emergency system.

She needs to feel safe with the staff working with her; emotional trauma responses are triggered when staff are unfriendly, demanding, judgmental, or demeaning in their manner. Evelyn is quick to feel and respond as though others may become abusive to her. She may use a behavioral event to attempt to protect herself, such as becoming aggressive toward staff when she believes that they are unkind and potentially hurtful.

MEDICAL ISSUES: Evelyn has high blood pressure and high cholesterol. She is on a low-cholesterol diet and sometimes becomes upset when she cannot eat the foods that she would like to eat.

HAPPINESS ANALYSIS:
- Pleasure: Evelyn loves to go out to eat. She also likes to watch romantic comedies.
- Engagement: Evelyn enjoys doing math problems and art work. Her favorite medium is colored pencils. She enjoys complex coloring books and also likes to use crayons and colored markers.
- Relationships: Evelyn cares very much about her friend Ellen at work and her boyfriend. She enjoys spending time with both of them.
- Achievements: Evelyn is proud of her ability to draw and has entered a local art show.
- Meaning: Evelyn's relationship with her boyfriend is very important to her. She enjoys spending the weekend at his place or having him over at her place. She wants very much to get married and be his wife.

HAPPINESS PROCEDURE:
- Procedure for pleasure increase: Evelyn should have an opportunity to go out to eat at least once a week. Evelyn should have a movie night at least twice a month and should be able to select the movies and invite friends.
- Procedure for engagement increase: Staff must keep art supplies on hand at home and math problems on hand at work for down times.
- Procedure for relationships: Staff should assist Evelyn in spending time with her friend Ellen at least two times per month.
- Procedure for achievement: Staff should assist Evelyn to obtain art supplies and explore her interests in art.

- Procedure for meaning increase: Staff should support the progression of Evelyn's relationship with her boyfriend. Staff should facilitate dating and further time spent together. If feasible, a vacation should be planned for them together rather than with separate housemates.

TRAUMA RESPONSE PREVENTION:

- Known triggers: Known triggers are running out of cigarettes, being around other people's children for more than 10 or 15 min, and holidays, particularly Christmas. Also, speaking in a loud tone and demanding or ordering rather than discussing on the part of staff is, at times, a trigger for Evelyn.
- Known difficult anniversaries: Christmas and her birthday. Evelyn has had particularly difficult times on her birthday.
- People who are trusted and available: Evelyn is very close to her associate director and to her house manager. She is also close to her therapist. She feels safe with these people and is able to become calm when upset if they are present.
- Choices that must be offered consistently: Evelyn must be allowed to choose her clothes and hair style; she resents fashions being put on her by staff. Evelyn should be allowed to make as many choices as possible. This is very important to her. As Evelyn's relationship with her boyfriend progresses, she and her boyfriend should be encouraged to choose whether to live together and which area to live in.
- Factors required to feel safe: Evelyn must have a supply of cigarettes, kept separately from her, at work and at home, as a backup when she runs out. Evelyn should also always have plans set for the Christmas holiday in advance, even if it is to be at home, and spend part of the day with her boyfriend; there should be a clear plan with activities to look forward to. The same should be done for her birthday, with a birthday celebration planned in advance. Plans should not be changed because of behavioral issues; instead, Evelyn should have extra therapy sessions if she becomes upset or agitated. Staff should remember to discuss, not demand, and to speak in a low, calm tone of voice.

POSITIVE IDENTITY DEVELOPMENT:

- Roles that are positive and staff support needed: Evelyn cares very much about her role as a girlfriend. She wants to be a caring and attentive girlfriend. Staff should talk to her about this role and assist her in girlfriend-like activities, such as getting her boyfriend a birthday gift, shopping for sexy nightwear, getting a makeover, using the phone correctly, and communicating with him about her feelings. Staff should coach her in these and other relevant girlfriend activities. Staff should praise and encourage all of her efforts and repeat the importance of this role to her.
- Actions staff must take to facilitate self-esteem: Staff should give Evelyn specific and accurate praise about her efforts and her ways. Staff should continually point out Evelyn's strong points and assist her in feeling pride about her strong points.

- Actions staff must take to facilitate positive peer relations: Evelyn should be encouraged to develop friendships and invite friends from work over for movies.

BEHAVIORAL INCIDENT PREVENTION:
- How to prevent behavioral difficulties when stressors/triggers occur:
  1. It is very important that staff be aware that Evelyn is triggered into a traumatic response when she does not have cigarettes. This response is completely out of proportion and likely to bring up years of feelings about loss and deprivation. The staff must have extra cigarettes on hand, hidden so that she does not smoke them, in both work and home settings. If possible, it would be helpful to encourage Evelyn to agree to a plan in which she could smoke on a schedule, with staff assistance, in order to make her supply last longer. This must be done with Evelyn's agreement.
  2. It is very important that Evelyn have a plan set at least 2 weeks ahead of time for activities on the holidays and on her birthday. Evelyn panics when she believes she will be alone and neglected at these times. This is very likely a trauma response from past neglect.
  3. Staff should speak in a soft, calm tone to Evelyn. If she feels she is being yelled at, she can be triggered into a highly emotional state. Staff must keep their voice calm and low.
  4. Staff should be careful to discuss any requirements, such as chore or hygiene completion, rather than demand in a parental or authoritarian mode. Evelyn is triggered through this approach and may become upset and agitated.
- How to prepare: All staff must be trained in the mental health plan before working with Evelyn.
- How to effectively redirect from negative to positive:
  1. If Evelyn is upset or agitated in any way, staff can often calm her down by suggesting that they let it go for now and plan a date night with her boyfriend. If it is cigarette related, staff must assist Evelyn in coming up with a plan for acquiring a cigarette. Again, staff should always keep backup cigarettes. Then staff can say, "Wait a minute! I think I saw one somewhere," and discreetly find one of the hidden cigarettes.
  2. If Evelyn is about to call 911, staff should remind her of the legal consequences of this act and ask her to let staff help her solve the problem first.
- How to respond when trauma triggers occur:
  1. If Evelyn is in a crisis state and remembering past hurts or overreacting to a situation, staff should quietly and calmly ground her in the present by reminding her that she is here now and that things are going to be okay. Then staff should calmly discuss the present issue in a way that helps Evelyn reach a solution.

2. If someone has triggered Evelyn, and Evelyn is targeting that person, staff should talk calmly to Evelyn and walk with her away from that person. Also, encourage the person to leave and not even attempt to discuss issues at that point. After 20 min of calming down, staff should discuss with Evelyn what she would like to do next and assist her in speaking with one of her safe people if available.

- What to do when anniversaries occur: As stated above, staff must have an advance plan that is appealing to Evelyn for birthdays and holidays.
- How to ensure a sense of safety:
  1. Evelyn should see her therapist weekly.
  2. Evelyn should choose with whom she lives.
  3. Evelyn should be allowed to tell administration when she does not like a staff person and feels uncomfortable and should get immediate assistance and resolution.
- How to monitor and report psychiatric concerns:
  1. Staff should report to the psychiatrists any changes in sleeping or eating as well as times when Evelyn appears to be responding to or listening to voices or seeing something no one else sees.
  2. Staff should report any changes in mood, particularly when Evelyn does not want to do what she normally enjoys or refuses to do what she typically doesn't mind doing.
- Therapeutic interventions required: Evelyn should see a therapist weekly. It is okay if the therapy takes place on location at home or work.

CRISIS INTERVENTION:
- How to emotionally connect in a stress situation:
  1. In a crisis, staff must first ask Evelyn, "What is really wrong, or what is really bothering you?" and push her to reveal her real emotion at the time. Then staff should discuss any immediate solution, such as how to get a cigarette, and long-term solutions, such as how to speak with an administrator about an unjust situation.
  2. Staff should calmly coax Evelyn into expressing her concerns to someone that she feels has power and should assist Evelyn in accessing this person or planning to access a person in power.
  3. Staff should discreetly get the phone so that Evelyn cannot call 911. If that is not possible, staff should call 911 after Evelyn has called to rectify the call.
- How to remove individual from a difficult situation:
  1. If Evelyn is upset with someone, staff should attempt to walk with Evelyn away from that person.
  2. If that is not possible, staff should ask the person to remove him- or herself away from Evelyn.

- Whom to contact to provide safety and connection:
    1. Evelyn's key people should be contacted, and someone should be accessed to talk with Evelyn. These people are the associate director, the house manager, and the therapist. The contact can be made by phone, or ideally in person.
    2. Evelyn should be allowed to talk with someone in the situation whom she feels will listen. Staff should ask her, "Who do you want to talk to right now of the people who are here?" Staff should offer to listen to her right then and there.
    3. Above all, staff must stay calm and unruffled and not indicate fear or anger.
- Criteria for hospitalization:
    1. If Evelyn is indicating that she is hearing voices or responding to internal stimuli, she should be taken to the hospital for psychiatric evaluation.
    2. If Evelyn is too emotional to speak and has become hysterical without being able to indicate why, she should be taken for evaluation.
- When to use community emergency services: If Evelyn is indicating that she intends, right in that moment, to hurt herself or someone else directly and she cannot be calmed or redirected after 3 to 5 min, call 911.

Style of Writing and Language Use

As you can see by this example, the writing style is kept simple and minimally clinical. It is important to remember when writing such a plan that the plan is meant to be read by individuals who may not have a college degree. It must be clear and understandable, yet at the same time address the very real, trauma-based issues that the individual has. It is important that clinicians simplify their style and approach the task as a challenge in basic communication of important concepts and complex direction. If the staff cannot understand the mental health plan, they can never implement it.

Example 2

Denny

Next, let us return to the first case history shared at the beginning of this book in Chapter 1. Denny was dropped off at an institution for individuals with developmental disabilities at age 4. He had little to no contact with his family, and at a very young age, he was completely at the mercy of a very unsupervised staff. At 44, he has difficulties with property destruction and aggression and has a behavior plan addressing these difficulties. More significantly, he suffers from acute stress disorder, which is a more intensified form of posttraumatic stress disorder. Denny is emotionally fragile and only minimally verbal. With this summary in mind, let's look at an example of a mental health plan that might be written for him.

MENTAL HEALTH PLAN

NAME: Denny Kohl

DATE OF BIRTH: 5/7/1957

LOCATION: Day and residential program

PLAN WRITER: Karyn Harvey

DATE: 02/02/2001

BACKGROUND: Denny was born in 1957 to George and Caroline Kohl. He showed indications of a developmental delay when motor activity and language development were significantly delayed, and he did not reach anticipated milestones by age 2. Information on Denny's actual development is scant. What is known is that Denny was dropped off at the X institution shortly before his 4th birthday at the recommendation of the family doctor. He was placed in the children's unit, where it is evident that he experienced repeated trauma. There is very little documentation of those events, but there are indications that Denny received several broken bones before age 12, and there was repeated use of restraints throughout the teenage years and into adulthood.

Denny came to the ABC residential agency at age 44 and entered the Z day program. He has been at these settings for some years and continues to exhibit signs of posttraumatic stress disorder. There continues to be no family involvement.

TRAUMA EXPERIENCES: It is clear that Danny underwent repeated physical abuse while institutionalized. He describes what he terms as being "messed up" by staff and exhibits and demonstrates an inordinate amount of fear toward older female staff. The records also indicate that he had a series of broken bones during his childhood years in the institution. There is no clear evidence of sexual abuse, but it may have occurred, based on general history of the setting that he resided in while in the institution.

DIAGNOSIS: Axis I: 308.3 acute stress disorder; Axis II: severe intellectual disability; Axis III: hypertension; Axis IV: history of physical abuse, institutionalization since childhood; Axis V: GAF: 30.

MEDICATION: Haldol, Depakote

EXPLANATION OF DIAGNOSIS: Acute stress disorder indicates that Denny underwent severe and repeated trauma that placed him in direct danger and had ongoing effects. People who have acute stress disorder sometimes have flashbacks and forget where they are and believe they are back at a traumatic time. They may also disconnect from themselves and not be entirely "there." They may also talk about themselves in the third person and, in extreme examples, act like different people. These are all signs that they have disconnected from themselves in some way as a result of the trauma that they experienced.

MEDICAL ISSUES: Denny has hypertension and has certain dietary restrictions.

HAPPINESS ANALYSIS:
- Pleasure: Denny loves to watch cartoons and listen to country music. Denny also loves Chinese food.
- Engagement: Denny enjoys jumping on a trampoline daily and taking walks with staff. He also likes to go to parties and interact with peers.
- Relationships: Denny has a friend Peter whom he also likes, and staff should assist Denny in spending time with him.
- Acheivements: Denny is proud of his clothes and ability to dress himself.
- Meaning: Denny is very close to his housemates. He is dear friends with one in particular, Johnny, who was with Denny in the institution. This friendship brings a great deal of comfort and meaning to Denny's life.

HAPPINESS PROCEDURE:
- Procedure for pleasure increase: Denny should have ample opportunities to watch cartoons on a television at home, regardless of what his housemates may want to watch. Denny should also have opportunities to listen to country music, perhaps on an iPod. Finally, Denny should be able to order Chinese food at least once a week, within the boundaries of his dietary restrictions.
- Procedure for engagement increase: Denny should have plenty of opportunities to go to parties within the residential agency and to socialize with friends. This is very important to him. He should also have opportunities to jump daily on the trampoline with staff supervision and take walks with staff and, if possible, with housemates, when he so chooses.
- Procedure for relationship maintenance: Denny should be encouraged to spend time with his friend Peter
- Procedure for achievement increase: Staff should make a big deal out of shopping for clothes and allow Denny to decide how he wants to look.
- Procedure for meaning increase: Staff should support Denny as much as possible in his friendship with his housemates. If possible, vacations together should be considered to create wonderful memories. Denny should actively choose preferred vacation sites and plan other activities with his housemates as well.

TRAUMA RESPONSE PREVENTION:
- Known triggers: Women over 50, who are blonde or light in hair color, are perceived as unsafe by Denny. Denny gets very upset when someone holds a belt in front of him or herself. Denny is also very afraid of hospitals and will refuse to go inside.
- Known difficult anniversaries: Denny withdraws and appears to become sad during the Christmas holiday. He does love punch and is cheered by that and gifts, but he often becomes depressed and withdrawn immediately after Thanksgiving and throughout the month of December.

- **People who are trusted and available:** Denny loves his housemate and his house manager, Latoya Johnson. Denny has known Bill James and Ellen Solor from the day program for a long time and indicates liking them very much. These are the people he appears to feel safest with.
- **Choices that must be offered consistently:** Denny should be encouraged to choose where he goes for outings on the weekends, what he watches on television, and, within his dietary restrictions, what he eats for the week. These choices are important to him.
- **Factors required to feel safe:** Denny needs to have his own room. It is evident that some sort of abuse occurred at night while in the institution. He does not like to share rooms with others, and he does not like to sleep without a nightlight. Denny should have a small light (a plug-in nightlight) in his room. Denny needs to be involved in the selection of staff, as he is usually not comfortable with middle-aged Caucasian women, which causes him anxiety, and can even trigger trauma responses in their presence. Denny does not like to ride in the front seat of the car—he sometimes becomes anxious when doing so. Denny likes to wear light clothes and does not like belts. He has a fear of belts and should not be around them.

  Denny feels safest when he knows the schedule for the day each day. If there is a change, Denny should be prepared for it in advance. Staff should talk in a soothing manner to Denny about any upcoming changes, including doctor's appointments, and prepare him in advance for it. Denny does not feel safe around loud voices. Staff should keep their voices low and talk to Denny in moderate tones. If staff are having a conflict, they should not have heated discussions in front of Denny as this will cause him undue anxiety.

POSITIVE IDENTITY DEVELOPMENT:
- **Roles that are positive and important to this person:** Denny is very proud of his role of best friend to his housemate. Denny is also proud of the envelope stuffing that he does at work. He is proud of this job and proud of the check that he earns. He does not have a clear sense of the amount of the money but enjoys cashing his check and having a wallet with several dollars in it at all times.
- **Actions staff must take to facilitate self-esteem:** Staff should praise Denny as being a good friend and good housemate to his housemates. Staff should praise specific helpful acts that Denny performs to assist his housemates. Staff should also praise Denny when he cashes his check for working so hard and earning money. At work, staff should encourage Denny on the days he works and let him know that he is a good worker.
- **Actions staff must take to facilitate positive peer relations:** Denny enjoys social activities with peers, and it would help Denny to expand his social circle. Therefore, staff should facilitate cookouts and occasional dinners out with friends for Denny. Staff should remind Denny how he is such a good friend and ask him

which other friends from work or his past that he would like to invite to these social events. This would assist Denny in seeing himself as someone who has a place in the social world.

BEHAVIORAL INCIDENT PREVENTION:
- How to prevent behavioral difficulties when stressors/triggers occur:
  1. Denny is triggered by conflicts between people. If there is a loud conflict at the work program or at home, staff should immediately comfort Denny. If possible, staff should try to take Denny to another location, by suggesting that they take a walk or, if at home, to go watch TV in another room. This should be done quickly so that Denny is not around the conflict for a long period of time.
  2. If Denny sees a belt, staff should put it away and tell him, "Don't worry, Denny, no belts around here. I will make sure everyone knows: no belts!" Then staff should reassure Denny that he is safe, everyone here is a friend, and the past is over.
  3. In general, if Denny becomes anxious, staff should verbally reassure him that he is safe and that the past is completely over. "Denny, you are here now and you are safe," should be repeated regularly to him.
  4. If Denny is around the type of woman who often triggers trauma responses, staff should immediately tell him her name and where she works and that she is nice and not at all like the staff from the institution.
- How to effectively redirect from negative to positive:
  1. If Denny is becoming upset, he can be redirected at home by watching his favorite cartoons. Staff should have these cartoons on DVD if possible.
  2. Denny must meet staff and interview them before they work with him.
  3. Denny should be able to listen to the music he likes when he is becoming anxious. Having an iPod would be ideal.
  4. Denny should be able to look forward to events. When he is upset, he can cheer up if he is reminded of an upcoming event. Staff should not, under any circumstances, threaten him by telling him that he will lose the opportunity to engage in this event.
- How to respond when trauma triggers occur:
  1. If Denny is going into his "trauma mind" or begins to have a glassy-eyed look and does not respond when staff reassure him, staff should tell him in a gentle voice that he is okay, he is fine, and they should remind him of where he is and that he is loved. Tell him again that he is loved and, if possible, offer him physical comfort, such as a pat on the arm or a hug.
  2. If possible, staff should try to encourage Denny to walk to another place and to be grounded in a familiar activity, such as eating a favorite snack or watching TV.

- **What to do when anniversaries occur:** Staff should have a special ritual for the Christmas holiday in the home and tell Denny that it's a new Christmas in the home. Staff should prepare Denny for the holiday and discuss the new rituals with excitement.
- **How to ensure a sense of safety:**
  1. Staff should always check in with Denny and make sure that he is feeling comfortable. Staff should pay attention to the list of triggers above, and provide Denny with constant reassurance that he is going to be fine and that things are okay.
  2. Staff should avoid reminders or references to Denny's life in the institution.
- **How to monitor and report psychiatric concerns:**
  1. Staff should report any change in sleep or eating habits to the psychiatrist.
  2. Staff should report any increase in anxiety or anxiety-related behaviors to the psychologist or to the psychologist associate.
  3. Staff should report any change in affect or lack of interest in usually enjoyable activities to the psychiatrist and psychology associate.
- **Therapeutic interventions required:**
  1. Denny would benefit from art therapy on a regular basis.
  2. It is recommended that Denny receive EMDR for trauma treatment from a trained EMDR therapist who has worked with individuals with ID or children.

CRISIS INTERVENTION:

- **How to emotionally connect in a stress situation:**
  1. Denny does best if a different person, one with whom he feels safe and comfortable but one who is not currently in the room, comes in and says something to Denny about an activity, such as an upcoming meal or activity that he can be redirected to. It is almost as though that different person is able to break some spell, a mental spell, so to speak, that Denny is under when he is in a traumatic state.
  2. If that is not possible, the staff person present should just talk calmly to Denny and bring him into the present by saying what the next event is—lunch, dinner, or whatever else—and how they are going to have a good time and how everything is fine and there is nothing to worry about right now. It is best to encourage Denny to leave the situation and take a walk or go elsewhere.
  3. If there is another individual with ID under stress and acting in a difficult manner, staff should suggest that Denny walk with them somewhere else to get Denny out of that situation.
  4. Denny responds best when staff talk in a soothing tone of voice about the future. Denny does not do well if staff rehash the situation over and over.
- **How to remove individual from a difficult situation:** As stated earlier, Denny does best to take a walk or go elsewhere when he has become upset or a crisis situation

is occurring. It is important that staff NOT touch Denny until he is completely calm. Denny can be touched only when he is not agitated.

- **Whom to contact to provide safety and connection:** Denny does best when his house manager or the associate director of the residential program is present. He also responds well to his day program instructor. Denny becomes more agitated when the day program director is present and when the executive director is present. The people whom Denny feels safe with may change, so staff should ask Denny and update the list of safe people for Denny.
- **Criteria for hospitalization:** If Denny remains out of touch with reality and mentions names of people who are not present or talks nonsensically, is physically aggressive or engaging in repeated property destruction and cannot be calmed down, he may need to be hospitalized.
- **When to use community emergency services:** If Denny cannot stop engaging in attempts at aggression or property destruction even after he is directed out of the situation, staff should contact 911.

Mental Health Plans for Little *t* Trauma

Both Examples 1 and 2 pertain to individuals who have endured complex trauma and either PTSD or acute stress disorder as a result. The mental health plan can also be useful to individuals who have had only the usual trauma associated with an adult life span and an intellectual disability. These little *t* traumas might include the experiences that individuals with ID often have in the public school system, such as incidents in the lunch room and hallways. It might also include the loss of family members , such as the deaths of grandparents or parents. These are normal traumas that most people experience, but the impact can be severe on someone with a cognitive disability who has a limited social network and limited access to emotional and psychological support.

I have met many individuals with ID who grieve the loss of a loved one for many many years, as though the loss had just occurred the day before. Greif is a source of trauma (Shapiro, 2001). People with ID often have very few significant relationships and when a parent or caretaker dies, it is not just a loss but a world shattered. Sometimes it is the loss of the only person who truly valued the individual. Peter's loss was significant when his father died.

He had been very close to his father and his father had been the patriarch for many years. Peter's mother was not as involved with him as his father. Peter lived at home. When his father died not only was his world decimated, his mother placed him in a residential agency immediately because she could not care for him. So Peter experienced the trauma of losing his father, his home, his daily routines, his mother's presence (because she rarely visited once he moved), and his entire life as her knew it. Sadly, I have seen this many times when families can no longer care for an individual with ID whom they have kept at home. The transition compounds the grief of the loss and there are those who never recover. Peter is fortunate to have a brother who is somewhat involved with him, but the other losses remain devastating.

Example 3

Peter

MENTAL HEALTH PLAN

NAME: Peter Spain

DATE OF BIRTH: 4/16/1967

LOCATION: Day and residential program

PLAN WRITER: Karyn Harvey

DATE: 09/10/2010

BACKGROUND: Peter was born in 1967 to Jake and Eileen Spain, the third of their four children. Peter has Down syndrome and a moderate intellectual disability. Peter was raised in his parents' home in Lutherville, Maryland, and attended public schools, where he received special education services. Peter was very involved in Special Olympics while growing up. Peter has two brothers and a sister; his brothers are older and his sister is younger. Peter was very close to his father while growing up. After receiving a certificate from school at age 21, Peter stayed home and helped his father with his landscaping business from time to time. Peter lived with his father and mother until age 40. When Peter was 40, his father died suddenly of a heart attack. Peter was present when his father died in their home. Peter's mother then felt that she was unable to care for Peter. Peter was transferred, 1 month after his father's death, to day and residential services and the X community-based agency. This transfer was very difficult for Peter. Peter expressed anger toward his mother and toward the staff. Peter remains very close to his brother, Bob, who visits him on a monthly basis.

TRAUMA EXPERIENCES: Peter experienced his father's sudden death as a trauma. He was very upset by the loss. He experienced the transition to residential and day services as a trauma as well, and is having difficulties adjusting. He did not think he would ever be placed in a program and was evidently promised by his father that this would never happen.

DIAGNOSIS: Axis I: V62.82 bereavement; Axis II: moderate intellectual disability; Axis III: Down syndrome, obesity; Axis IV: significant recent loss and significant and abrupt transition in living situation; Axis V: 35.

MEDICATION: Prozac

EXPLANATION OF DIAGNOSIS: Bereavement means that Peter is grieving his father in a manner in which his mental health is affected. Peter is mourning the loss of his father, that friendship, and also the life that he had when his father was alive. He talks extensively about activities that he and his father used to do. Staff report that he often cries late at night. Down syndrome, the genetic disorder that Peter has, predisposes him to depression.

MEDICAL ISSUES: Peter is obese and would benefit from improvements in diet and exercise. Peter has Down syndrome and therefore needs to be watched for early onset of Alzheimer's and any possible heart problems, sleep apnea, and digestive problems, which are all associated with Down syndrome.

HAPPINESS ANALYSIS:
- **Pleasure:** Peter enjoys going to the movies, eating out, particularly at Denny's, and watching action movies at home.
- **Engagement:** Peter is an avid bowler. He was in a bowling league in the past and has said that he would like to join one again. Peter also likes to do woodworking. According to his brother, Peter did woodworking with his father for many years and particularly enjoyed making birdhouses.
- **Relationships:** Peter enjoys being with his brother and brother's family as well as spending time with his friend Denny.
- **Acheivement:** Peter is proud of the deck that he helped his Dad build in their old home and loves to discuss things he has built.
- **Meaning:** Peter cares very much about his family. His mother is now ill, and it is very difficult for him to see her as often as he would like, but these visits are very important to him. He is very close to his brother, Bob, and looks forward to seeing Bob each month.

HAPPINESS PROCEDURE:
- **Procedure for pleasure increase:** Peter should have many opportunities to go to the movies and to rent or order movies. This is a much-loved activity for him. He should also have regular opportunities to go to Denny's with staff and friends. Staff should encourage Peter to choose the night and arrange to go to Denny's with the friends whom he would like to go with.
- **Procedure for engagement increase:** Staff should arrange for Peter to be on a bowling league. It would be ideal to find a league in which Peter could bowl with at least one or two individuals whom he knows. Peter also might enjoy a beginners' woodworking class if there is one available in the adult education program near his new home. It is important for Peter to be engaged in enjoyable activities. The more he is engaged in such activities, the less he is consumed with grief over the death of his father or the loss of living in his family's home.

Peter should have as many opportunities as possible to engage in activities and make new friends.

- **Procedure for relationship maintenance:** As stated earlier staff should assist Peter in seeing his friend Denny on a regular basis.
- **Procedure for achievement increase:** Staff should explore assisting Peter in developing his woodwork abilities.
- **Procedure for meaning increase:** It is important for staff to assist Peter in seeing his mother. His mother is not very mobile, and this will take some effort on staff's part. Staff should assist Peter in being available for visits with his brother as well.

TRAUMA RESPONSE PREVENTION:

- **Known triggers:** Peter becomes very upset when other people with whom he works at the day program talk about spending time with their fathers. He also becomes upset when the individuals who work but live at home talk about living with their parents. Peter should be encouraged by staff at these moments—it is ideal if someone can take him for a walk and listen to and celebrate his memories.
- **Known difficult anniversaries:** Peter gets upset on Father's Day; on 10/13, which is his father's birthday; and on Christmas. These are his most difficult times, during which he should either be with his brother or receive extra staff support.
- **People who are trusted and available:** Peter can be comforted quickly by talking with his brother Bob. He is also very close to his house manager, James Pratt. He has not yet formed close relationships at the day program.
- **Choices that must be offered consistently:** Peter should be allowed to choose whom he lives with and which day program site he wants to attend. This is very important to him.
- **Factors required to feel safe:** Peter was alone in the bathroom when he heard the noises of his father's death. To this day, he sometimes becomes upset after being in the bathroom and will talk repeatedly about the event. Staff should be available to him and nearby when he is using the bathroom.

POSITIVE IDENTITY DEVELOPMENT:

- **Roles that are positive and staff support needed:** Peter is very proud of his role of brother and uncle to his brother's children. Visits from his brother and wife and visits to see the family mean a great deal to Peter. Peter is also proud of his job working with plants. He will talk a great deal about the work that he does when asked. This is an important and positive aspect of his identity. Staff should assist in helping Peter to connect with his brother and get needed transportation for visits.
- **Actions staff must take to facilitate self-esteem:** Staff should praise Peter for being a great brother and uncle after he interacts with family. They should also praise all efforts that he makes toward his mother. He appears to be afraid of her death and sometimes avoids her, so staff should understand that all the efforts

he makes to see or call his mother should be supported by staff, and he should be praised for being a caring son.

In addition, Peter loves to show people some of the plants that he has grown. A trip by staff to the horticultural work site every 3 or 4 months or so would be a great boost for Peter. Allow some time for him to show what he has been growing and explain the plant-growing process that he has been engaged in.

- **Actions staff must take to facilitate positive peer relations:** Peter has a tendency to isolate himself or to only want to be with staff when at home. Staff should encourage outings and ask Peter which friends from work he might like to invite. Staff should support and encourage any social connections that Peter may want to make or show an interest in. Peter isolated himself a great deal during the mourning period; too much isolation is not healthy for him at this point, and staff may need to strongly encourage and assist Peter in making friends with peers.

BEHAVIORAL INCIDENT PREVENTION:

- **How to prevent behavioral difficulties when stressors/triggers occur:** Peter is triggered by people referring to their own fathers in the context of recent time spent with their fathers. It would be wise to ensure that there are special plans for Father's Day. Peter is also sometimes jealous and sad when someone who works at the horticulture program leaves with family or has a family visit with a mother and father. These are times when it would be helpful for staff to spend time with Peter after the person leaves with his or her family. Staff can just be by his side and do not necessarily have to talk about the incident or Peter's feelings. He often just benefits from the comfort of the physical presence of a staff member for whom he cares.
- **How to prepare:** All staff must be trained in Peter's mental health plan before working with him.
- **How to effectively redirect from negative to positive:** If Peter is becoming upset, it might be helpful for staff to direct him to a simple task and praise his ability to do that task. This is especially helpful at work, where Peter takes pride in the work that he does. At home, Peter enjoys action movies and can be redirected to watching a movie or to listening to some of his favorite pop music CDs.
- **How to respond when trauma triggers occur:** If Peter is becoming upset and talking about his father or his mother, staff should take a walk with him and listen to him talk about his memories. This is very helpful for Peter. If he is ignored, he usually becomes more and more upset. Staff need to spend time alone with him and let him talk about feelings and share memories at these times.
- **What to do when anniversaries occur:** Staff should plan special events for Father's Day to redirect and support Peter. Staff should assist the family with whatever is necessary in order to continue having Peter share holidays with his brother and his family.

- **How to ensure a sense of safety:** If Peter is highly upset, and/or crying a great deal, staff should not leave him alone and should sit with him and listen to him until he is calm. Staff should also be nearby when he is alone in the bathroom.
- **How to monitor and report psychiatric concerns:**
  1. Staff should report any change in sleep or eating habits to the psychiatrist.
  2. Staff should report any change in affect or lack of interest in usually enjoyable activities to the psychiatrist and psychology associate.
- **Therapeutic interventions required:** Peter should continue with weekly counseling with an emphasis on grief therapy.

CRISIS INTERVENTION:
- **How to emotionally connect in a stress situation:**
  1. When Peter is very upset about the loss of his father, he is comforted by the promise of interaction with his brother and his brother's family. If staff listen to him and comfort him and then mention a phone call to the brother or a visit with him, Peter is comforted. Peter does not go into crisis mode unless he feels he is being ignored or there is further bad news.
  2. If Peter's mother passes away or becomes very ill, staff should be ready to give Peter extensive emotional support, and the therapist should be contacted.
- **How to remove individual from a difficult situation:** If Peter is engaging in property destruction, staff should tell him that they will wait for him to finish and stand by. Peter is most likely to stop and discuss his feelings if they remain present and attentive.
- **Whom to contact to provide safety and connection:** As stated above, Peter's brother is the person to contact when Peter is upset. At this point, he is willing to be contacted on his cell phone. If he is unavailable, Peter's house manager should be contacted, and he will be able to speak with Peter and give emotional support. The therapist is also a backup source of emotional support and is available by cell phone.
- **Criteria for hospitalization:** The only circumstances in which psychiatric hospitalization may be required is if Peter has indicated that he wants to hurt himself or kill himself. Notify the on-call psychology associate immediately.
- **When to use community emergency services:** If Peter has attempted or is in the process of attempting to hurt himself seriously or kill himself, 911 should be contacted.

Little *t* Trauma: The Trauma of Invalidation

In Chapter 6, I discussed the trauma of invalidation. I believe that being discounted is a small but traumatic experience, one that people with intellectual disability have again and again. The invalidation I am referring to is to be told that you have not experienced what you just experienced, that the reality you witnessed never occurred.

For example, many individuals with ID who have been sexually molested have been told that they were not molested. In my experience as a therapist working with individuals with ID, these individuals' abuse experiences were often discounted by family members. Although they experienced abuse, they were told they did not experience it. The abuse itself is traumatic with a big *T*. However, the invalidation is also traumatic.

The invalidation often continues after placement in a community agency. Staff sometimes feel empowered to inform the individuals with whom they are working that these individuals are not really feeling certain ways. For example, pains that cannot be proven are often seen as invalid or faked. Individuals with head injuries will have pains that are phantom from time to time. Or when individuals are upset because they have been directly insulted, they are often told that there was no insult, even though there was. Having one's own experience be discounted can cause confusion and, more deeply, doubt and shame. This, in itself, is a little *t* trauma.

Example 4

Sharon

Sharon had experienced such a trauma when she was told by her mother that she was never sexually abused. She recalled being repeatedly sexually abused as a child by her stepfather and reporting it to her mother. The response from her mother was that Sharon was wrong. This happens to children and adults with ID regularly, in my experience. Something is done to them and then, after they report it, they are told that they are wrong, it didn't happen. Because individuals with ID are so powerless, perpetrators and their enablers can get away with this approach. This leaves the victim reeling, questioning whether or not her perception was correct.

Such a thing happened to Sharon. In addition to not feeling valued as a human being, she constantly questioned her perceptions throughout the rest of her life. The sexual abuse she endured was dealt with in therapy, and the trauma was worked through. However, Sharon had an ongoing doubt of the reality of her feelings and her experiences. That self-doubt pervaded every aspect of her life, and she went through periods of extreme dependency on staff, which would be peppered with outbursts of anger and rebellion when she attempted to assert the validity of her feelings. At these times, she would be labeled by staff as someone who was "having a behavior" and "being bad." When she would revert back to dependency, accepting her experience of anger as invalid as well, she would be praised for being good. This is a cycle I have frequently observed among individuals with ID.

The behavior modification plan written for Sharon addresses her outbursts of verbal aggression and her occasional physical aggression. The plan used to address promiscuous behavior as well, but she worked through that issue in therapy and is able to stay in one relationship at a time. The behavior plan further reduced her to "bad Sharon," whose feelings are not valid, and "good Sharon," who is able to suppress and collaborate in the denial of her emotions and experiences. A mental health plan would, instead, help Sharon to be able to develop a more meaningful life and to be frank and open about her feelings without having to express them in periodic eruptions that ultimately caused her shame. It would refocus the staff on understanding her emotions and her experience rather than regarding her as a "behaving entity" whose behavior needed to be controlled. Staff could relax their attempts to control her and shift instead to a supporting mode.

MENTAL HEALTH PLAN

NAME: Sharon Newman

DOB: 2/13/1984

LOCATION: Residential and work settings

PLAN WRITER: Karyn Harvey

DATE: 03/04/2010

BACKGROUND: Sharon Newman was born to Lisa and John Newman in Hagerstown, Maryland. She was the first of their three daughters. A developmental delay was detected at age 3 by the family physician, when Sharon had not reached the significant milestones of speech development. Sharon's facial features were observed to resemble those of an individual with fetal alcohol syndrome, but this syndrome has not been confirmed. Sharon was placed in a residential school at age 12 following parental complaints about behavioral issues, including periodic aggression. While at school, Sharon revealed that she had been sexually abused on three separate occasions by her father. These allegations were denied by the family, and the evidence was no longer available. The abuse was basically discounted.

Sharon remained in the residential placement until age 21 when she transferred to the X agency. There she received day and residential services. Sharon's parents divorced when she was 13. She no longer has contact with her father. Sharon's mother continues to remain involved in her life and will have her to her home every 2 or 3 months and for holidays. Sharon has remained at the X agency and has been successful in her residential and supported employment placements.

TRAUMA EXPERIENCES: Sharon was sexually abused by her father; on every level this allegation appears to be true. Her therapist confirms very real memories and associated feelings. Sharon has also been traumatized by the divorce of her parents and subsequent absence of her father. In addition, Sharon continues to be upset by the fact that her family does not believe that she was ever sexually abused.

DIAGNOSIS: Axis I: none; Axis II: 301.83 borderline personality disorder, 317 mild intellectual disability; Axis III: obesity; Axis IV: history of sexual abuse, family difficulties; Axis V: GAF: 50.

MEDICATION: Prozac

EXPLANATION OF DIAGNOSIS: Individuals with a borderline personality disorder often have an insatiable need for love, attention, and drama. Many people with borderline personality disorders have been sexually abused as children; through this experience they were rewarded for lying and experienced unnatural intimacy at a young age. As a result, they may fabricate or lie, they may often crave intimacy and thus create crises so that people will rush to them and be close, and they may have patterns of promiscuity or flirtation. The pattern fits Sharon and people working with her should understand the roots of her attention-seeking actions in the early experience of sexual abuse.

MEDICAL ISSUES: Sharon struggles with obesity and requires staff assistance to accept and implement calorie control.

HAPPINESS ANALYSIS:
- Pleasure: Sharon loves to go out to eat, enjoys going to the moves, and likes watching reality shows.
- Engagement: Sharon enjoys bowling, more for the socializing with the league she is a part of than the actual sport; going to parties; meeting friends for dinner; and having guests over to her home. Her social life is a form of enjoyment and engagement.
- Relationships: Sharon cares very much about her friends and should have the opportunity to spend time with those friends.
- Achievements: Sharon is proud of her job and the work that she periodically does, this helps to build a sense of positive identity. She is also proud of her appearance.
- Meaning: Sharon finds a great deal of meaning in the time that she is able to spend with her family and the gifts that she is able to buy for them with her earned money. She also finds meaning in her relationship with her boyfriend; she wants very much to be married to him and finds meaning in her future role as wife.

HAPPINESS PROCEDURE:
- Procedure for pleasure increase: Sharon should have an opportunity to go out to dinner at least once a week. In addition, staff should assist her in attending a movie at least one time per month. Sharon has requested a TV in her room, so that she can watch the reality shows that she enjoys while everyone else watches

the Lifetime channel. Staff should take action to assist Sharon in saving for and purchasing a small TV for her room.

- **Procedure for engagement increase:** Staff should secure transportation to the parties that Sharon enjoys and to the bowling league. In addition, staff should assist Sharon in having dinner with friends and inviting friends to her home periodically.
- **Procedure for relationship maintenance:** Staff should assist Sharon in seeing both her girlfriends and her boyfriend on weekends.
- **Procedure for achievement increase:** Staff should assist Sharon in enhancing her appearance and engaging in doing nails, hair, and the like.
- **Procedure for meaning increase:** Staff should help to facilitate dates between Sharon and her boyfriend. In addition, staff should support family visits for Sharon and should never advise the family that Sharon was not "good enough" to go home or that she had not "earned the visit." Staff should instead help to arrange the visits and keep them going by maintaining positive contact with the family.

TRAUMA RESPONSE PREVENTION:

- **Known triggers:** If Sharon is caught in a demanding situation and unable to respond appropriately, she might begin to lie and then lie more; the lies themselves then become triggers, and she becomes anxious and upset. It is possible that this was a pattern during the period of sexual abuse and that lying itself triggers a panic response, even though she does it compulsively when under stress.
- **Known difficult anniversaries:** For reasons unknown, Sharon often becomes agitated and even, at times, disruptive in the days before her birthday. She appears to be anxious that she will be forgotten and possibly upset by memories and associations.
- **People who are trusted and available:** Sharon is very close to the house manager, to her job instructor, and to her boyfriend. She feels safe with these people and will, after having lied, often tell them the truth.
- **Choices that must be offered consistently:** Sharon must be able to have some say over her weekend activities. It is very important to her to be social and engaged over the weekend and to be a part of setting the weekend activities up with staff and friends.
- **Factors required to feel safe:** Sharon feels safe when people listen to her and allow her to speak a great deal about her feelings and activities. Sharon becomes unhappy and may lie or fabricate situations to get people to listen to her if she does not have daily talk time with staff (several times per day is preferable). After that, Sharon no longer appears to need to create situations. Listening is critical for her; the more staff listen to her, the safer and happier she appears to feel.

POSITIVE IDENTITY DEVELOPMENT:

- **Roles that are positive and staff support needed:** Sharon feels very proud of the work that she does at her job. Staff at work and at home should continue praising these efforts. Sharon is also proud of her role of girlfriend and looks forward to being a wife. Staff should encourage and support Sharon in the development of her relationship skills.

- **Actions staff must take to facilitate self-esteem:** Sharon responds well to specific praise. Sharon enjoys learning new skills. Although she may take a considerable amount of time to learn these skills, she will eventually learn them, and once she has mastered a new skill, she is very proud and excited. Staff should invest as much teaching time with Sharon as possible.
- **Actions staff must take to facilitate positive peer relations:** Sharon is very social and will invite friends to the home and out for activities if given staff support. These social activities as well as activities with her boyfriend mean a great deal to her and should be encouraged. This also helps to build her positive self-identity as she views herself as a friend to others and also as girlfriend to her significant other.

BEHAVIORAL INCIDENT PREVENTION:
- **How to prevent behavioral difficulties when stressors/triggers occur:**
    1. Sharon becomes very upset when she is caught in a lie. If staff catch her in a lie and confront her in an unfriendly manner, she will become emotional and explosive. If Sharon is lying, staff should not confront her in front of others. Rather, they should listen to her and later on, in private, ask her what is really going on. They should then encourage her in understanding that she can come to staff with problems or issues, even small issues, without having a big crisis. Also, staff should try to communicate to Sharon that she is accepted as she is, is okay as she is, and does not need a crisis or drama to receive attention or care.
    2. If Sharon is rejected by a male, a possible boyfriend, for example, this rejection will often trigger a trauma response of either attempts at superficial self-injury or promiscuity. It is important that staff be empathetic and spend special time with Sharon if any rejection occurs, such as a girls' day of getting nails done and shopping, or whatever may comfort Sharon. When this is done, she usually is able to recover from such rejection.
- **How to effectively redirect from negative to positive:** If Sharon is lying or becomes promiscuous, staff should focus on the positive and direct her to enjoying girls' activities, such as getting her hair done, shopping, or going to a fun movie, and not dwell on the negative. Sharon's therapist should be communicated with, and Sharon should receive opportunities for additional therapy. If there is any self-injury, the therapist should be contacted immediately. Sharon is greatly comforted by female bonding activities and also responds well to therapy.
- **How to prepare:** Staff should be thoroughly trained in Sharon's plan before working with her. In addition, they should be prepared to diffuse and redirect the beginnings of any crises that Sharon may attempt to produce. Staff should

have a list of interests and activities to redirect Sharon to when she begins to become upset.

- **How to respond when trauma triggers occur:**
  1. If Sharon has a conflict with her family, staff should contact the therapist and arrange for Sharon to be able to see the therapist for a session or to talk with the therapist, if possible, on the phone. Staff should listen to Sharon without taking sides against the family or for them but, instead, use active listening skills to process Sharon's feelings and support the validity of her feelings. This is very important.
  2. If Sharon is rejected in any way, by a job, boyfriend, or friend, staff should take the time to spend special one-on-one time with Sharon and to nurture her as much as possible through the emotions associated with being rejected.
- **What to do when anniversaries occur:** Sharon should have special plans with staff for her birthday, set in advance.
- **How to ensure a sense of safety:**
  1. Sharon should see her therapist on a regular basis, to be determined by the therapist.
  2. Sharon should be allowed to see her boyfriend and supported in this relationship by staff.
  3. If Sharon has had a difficult conversation with her mother, staff should spend extra one-on-one time with Sharon and support her. The same should occur if there are problems with her boyfriend, because these are the times that Sharon is in the most danger of self-injuring.
- **How to monitor and report psychiatric concerns:** Staff should report any change in sleeping or eating to the psychiatrist. Staff should also report if Sharon loses interest in what she normally enjoys doing or if she no longer wants to socialize with friends or see her family or boyfriend. This has occurred once, around the time of the Christmas holiday, when Sharon exhibited signs of depression.
- **Therapeutic interventions required:** Sharon should see a therapist regularly, and increased sessions should be added if self-injury or lying increase.

CRISIS INTERVENTION:
- **How to emotionally connect in a stress situation:** When Sharon is upset she likes to talk about how she looks. She responds well to compliments and may connect with someone who assists her in feeling good about her appearance.
- **How to remove individual from a difficult situation:**
  1. If staff come upon Sharon in a high-risk sexual situation, staff should not raise their voice but should calmly ask Sharon to get herself together and speak with staff privately. It is important that Sharon not be humiliated. Staff should allow Sharon to reflect on her own behavior and should encourage Sharon to remember her goals and the rules of safety and to take action to follow her own goals.

2. If Sharon is upset and cutting herself or superficially injuring herself, staff should interrupt her immediately, apply appropriate first aid, contact the on-call individuals, and discuss with her what is bothering her. Staff should also arrange a therapy session. Staff should not arrange an immediate psychiatry session for a change in medication but should address the issue as though it is emotionally, not psychiatrically based.

- **Whom to contact to provide safety and connection:** Sharon appears to feel safe with her house manager, job instructor, and boyfriend. She should be able to talk with her house manager as soon as can be arranged if she is having difficulty during the day. She should be able to see her boyfriend within a day or two of a difficult time. Staff should support these connections and facilitate face-to-face time.
- **Criteria for hospitalization:** Although Sharon has not needed hospitalization for psychiatric issues thus far, contact her therapist if there is a question based on signs of depression or occurrence of self-injury in a serious or repeated manner.
- **When to use community emergency services:** Sharon has not yet needed 911 to be contacted for any psychiatric emergencies. The on-call emergency line for the agency should be contacted in any psychiatric emergency first and allowed to make the determination whether to contact 911.

Mental Health Plans for Individuals with Borderline Personality Disorders

All the individuals with whom I have worked who have been diagnosed with a borderline personality disorder (BPD) have experienced trauma. The majority of those with whom I have worked have had mild intellectual disability and have experienced sexual abuse. The rare exceptions who were not sexually abused experienced serious medical trauma between the ages of 1 and 6. They were all exposed to excessive adult attention. They were the focus of adult attention in an abnormal manner. Once exposed to that level of attention, either through hospital care or through an illicit and abusive sexual relationship, they began to crave that level of attention.

Individuals who were sexually abused, like Sharon, were rewarded for lying and were told, in many cases, that they had a "special love." How horrible it must be to find out that it was merely abuse for physical gratification. These individuals who might have assumed they were special and dearly loved due to their bodily availability came to find out that they were no longer needed and not so special. In some cases, others took their place; in other cases, the offenders went to jail. Those who had excessive medical needs may have recovered and been surprised when they no longer received a great deal of attention. My experience has been that these individuals develop an insatiable need for intimacy through interaction and attention that carries into adulthood.

Intimacy does not necessarily mean sex or sexual relations. It may mean merely having the level of focus of attention that they were once used to and came to crave.

What creates such intimacy? Certainly a crisis does. An accusation of abuse, a need, a want, a loss that becomes magnified—all call for a high level of intimacy and attention. The people with whom I have worked who had BPD seemed to fit this model of having an insatiable hunger for intimacy and attention and a history of abuse or, in rare cases, extreme medical problems when young. Of course, not all people with BPD have been sexually abused or have had early medical difficulties. In a review of the literature, Paris (2008) concluded that abuse is a risk factor for BPD. Soloff, Lynch, and Kelly (2002) found that patients with BPD have a significantly higher incidence of sexual abuse than patients with other *DSM* diagnoses.

The most important point, however, when working with individuals with BPD and ID is to understand that there is a high likelihood of childhood trauma and, in particular, childhood sexual trauma. It is important that we do not focus on the symptoms of the sexual abuse as manifested in a personality disorder and treat only those symptoms. In other words, we must address whatever underlying trauma is at the root of the symptoms. For years, individuals with ID and BPD were treated as highly manipulative. Very structured behavioral support plans were used to control and reduce the lying and crisis-inducing behaviors. Instead of gaining total control, such interventions merely incited endless power struggles and, frequently, the appearance of new and more creative behavioral issues. BPD needs to be seen as an emotional disorder, very often tied to trauma experiences.

In many cases, individuals with BPD and ID fit the profile of someone in trauma mind. These individuals often revert back to the age of trauma and may place staff and others in parental roles as they act out the role of child. These role plays often involve high drama. As staff are empowered to recognize trauma and the recovery process, they will learn to enable individuals to break out of these patterns and move into the present.

References

Paris, J. (2008). *Treatment of borderline personality disorder*. New York: Guilford Press.

Shapiro, F. (2001). *Eye movement desensitization and reprocessing (EDMR): Basic principles, protocols, and procedures*. New York: Guilford Press.

Snyder, C. R., & Lopez, S. J. (2007). *Positive psychology: The scientific and practical explorations of human strengths*. Thousand Oaks, CA: Sage.

Soloff, P. H., Lynch, K. G., & Kelly, T. M. (2002). Childhood abuse as a risk factor for suicidal behavior in borderline personality disorder. *Journal of Personality Disorders, 16*, 201–214.

Programmatic Services from a Trauma-Informed Perspective

I magine a community-based agency where every individual who came to it was assessed for level and degree of trauma, and services were set up to support that person so that he or she felt safe, connected to others, and empowered. When an incident occurred, instead of plying the individual with medication or treating the individual like a bad child, an analysis could be done. This analysis could entail examining which triggers were present, how the individual may have felt unsafe, and how the individual may have been alienated from important connections or experienced possible perceptions of powerlessness and lack of control. After such an analysis was done, that individual's team could work together to put back in place those factors needed for that person to feel safe, connected, and empowered.

Even positive behavioral supports focus the staff on the individual's behaviors rather than on the individual. It is far better to be positive about behavioral control than to use restrictive and demeaning techniques, but the focus is still not on who the individual is and what he or she needs on an individual basis in order to become happy.

If we maintain the Judith Herman (1997) model of the triangle of safety, connection, and empowerment as a model for services, we can enable individuals to recover from both big T and little t trauma as well as to move forward and focus on their happiness and growth. This recovery model is ideal for programmatic applications. If we are to serve someone within a community-based agency, or similar structure, we should examine this triangle in all aspects of services (see Figure 2).

Safety

Safety is critical. Individuals must feel safe in their own homes, first and foremost. Sadly, too many of the people whom I have worked with and served did not feel safe in their own homes and were, thus, unable to benefit from therapeutic or behavioral interventions. Nothing works if an individual does

FIGURE 2 Recovery Model

Ingredients Necessary for Recovery

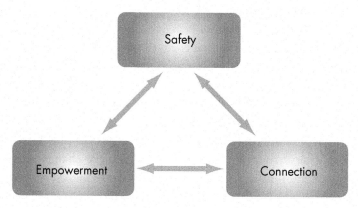

not feel safe. Herman (1997) asserted this over and over again. No one can begin to heal if they do not feel safe.

Sometimes, behind closed doors, staff threaten individuals: "If you don't clean up, I will [do X]," or "I told you what I would do to you if you did that one more time," and so on. When staff are not adequately trained in the emotional needs of the people they work with and when staff are made to feel that it is their job to control the behaviors of the people they serve, they may become desperate and slip into parental mode without realizing it. We psychologists give staff the message that we expect them to keep behaviors under control. Many of us revert back to the methods by which we were raised when attempting to assert control over others.

No one who is threatened can ever feel safe.

No one who is spoken to in a demeaning or controlling manner in their own home can truly relax in that home.

No one who is maligned in any way on a daily basis can begin to heal.

In the day programs or at work sites, individuals may be subjected to teasing or bullying of some kind by other co-workers. This is a common occurrence. I have witnessed occasions when staff, rather than intervening, chime in. How can an individual feel safe in his or her workplace when there is a constant threat of humiliation or attack? There is no safety in such circumstances. Again, at that point, many individuals with ID may revert to fight, flight, or freeze mode. At that point, behavior plans are implemented and everyone discusses that individual's maladaptive or challenging behaviors. We rarely examine whether that individual feels safe in his or her workplace and is safe enough to grow and develop in a healthy manner vocationally. Without feeling safe, that person cannot demonstrate his or her full potential. The executive functioning aspects of the brain are silent when an individual is in fight, flight, or freeze mode.

Empowerment

There is real choice, and there is fake choice. Asking people what they would like to do with their lives, congratulating them for saying it, and recording it in a document is not real choice. Real choice includes being able to quit a job, being able to change residences without having to ask for that change every day for 5 or 6 years. Real choice involves knowing who you are, what you want, and how to initiate change.

Many of the individuals with whom I have worked throughout the years assert choices and try to create change in their lives by desperate actions. Joe, for example, asked to move many, many times. In frustration one day, Joe threw furniture and engaged in property destruction. Then Joe was soon moved. This is the scenario we often see. People are driven to desperate actions to make change actually happen. Words aren't enough in many agencies. Those who can't talk can still express preferences. When we teach individuals with ID that the only way to make change happen is through negative actions, we are reinforcing old behavioral models and teaching them that we respond only to their extreme acts, not to their requests and preferences.

Empowerment is about real choice. It is the right to choose to change your life. It is the right to chose who you live with and the right to choose relationships. Many individuals who are adults with ID have limited recreation. Others have recreation that is not of their choosing. Still others live their staff's life while riding in the back seat of the car. This is not choice.

No choice is tantamount to no power. No power, according to Herman (1997), means no hope and ability to heal from trauma. Many of the folks we serve are stuck in some in-between place of living in which their entire life is structured by those around them with very little input from them. Behind closed doors, many staff are determining the day-to-day activities of individuals without their input or preference being considered. Lack of resources, lack of training, and lack of awareness are all the culprits (McLaughlin & Wehman,1992).

However, if you spent your entire life following others around, doing what they determined you would do, and following their instructions, you would lose the ability to take initiative or make choices. Just because people don't protest doesn't mean that they wouldn't love to direct their lives. Imagine living under the direction of others your entire life and then dying—never to determine the direction you wanted your life, let alone your day, to go in. This is the way of life for many individuals with ID. No wonder they often do not recover from trauma that occurred years and years ago.

Connections

According to Herman (1997), a person who lives in emotional isolation cannot begin the healing process. Connections to others through relationships are both the window to the world and a mirror of the self. Daniel Siegel (2010) wrote about true consciousness occurring at the point where two minds meet in relationship. We are validated by our connections with others. According to Siegel, that is when we are most conscious and aware of our own existence: when we are making a mental connection with another human being on a meaningful level.

There has been a movement in the field of ID to promote connections between people with ID and people in the community (Wolfensberger, 2011). Although this is a very exciting prospect in theory, the result is often that community-based agencies start to believe that somehow the individuals whom we serve will make connections in the community on their own and find their own friends and relationships. Sadly, this usually does not happen. Instead, agencies that assume such connections are occurring do not make the effort or communicate the importance to staff of connecting the individuals to their friends and facilitating the making of new friends. It is difficult to have a social life when you do not control your own transportation.

We cannot assume that the kind members of the church or neighbors in the community are reaching out to the individuals with ID in the normal course of their lives. This may occur here and there as an exception, but in our society, it is not the rule. Program administrators and psychologists need to examine how relationships between individuals with ID can be enhanced. We also need to assist in the facilitation of love and romance. Individuals who are not empowered do not initiate connections. We need to ask ourselves how we can start a chain of connections or increase that chain programmatically in a way that staff and individuals can easily continue.

Relationships become programmatic issues. They are issues of advancement; they are choice and connection. We should allow people and, in fact, assist people in being able to date, have relationships, and learn about themselves and others through those connections as well. Agencies have the resources to facilitate this and many do. Other agencies, however, are afraid to encourage love and sex, even friendship.

Programmatic Romance

When an agency is committed to the happiness of the individuals it serves, that agency finds ways to support relationships between individuals. Love and sex require education. We should not be afraid of pregnancies; we should be educating people and facilitating informed choices. Many couples with disabilities whom I know chose not to have children after being fully educated on the financial, physical, and mental commitment required. Yet they were able to find ways to work out their relationships and, in many cases, marry.

An excellent role for the psychologist or psychology associate, who will no longer have so many behavior plans to write once people are safe, empowered, and connected, is to offer couples counseling. I have found that techniques used for individuals without disabilities work just as well with individuals with ID when a more concrete level of communication is facilitated by the therapist.

If the agency is able to support the individual in establishing and maintaining relationships, both romantic and friendship based, the agency will find that it will save costs in extra staffing, behavioral interventions, and staff turnover. Individuals who are happy, who have friends and partners, need far less staff support. And staff quit less when the people they serve are happy and easy to work with. This is something we all know from working in this field. Increased and enhanced relationships between individuals with ID increase connection and create a viable and effective social network.

There are those individuals who often do not want to be in relationships with others with ID. That is fine. Some may choose to seek relationships with people in the community. Others may, in fact, prefer to be alone. That is fine, too. Let's use our resources, however, to provide real choices, not fake ones based on ideas about relationships. Then the people we serve can make true choices and true connections.

Programmatic Friendships

Although most community agencies both nonprofit and state-run are, at the time of this writing, feeling the sting of budget cuts, there are still decisions that can be made about allocations of funds and administrative job descriptions. Part of the allocation or job descriptions of certain positions can focus on increasing social opportunities for the individuals whom we are serving. If the culture of the organization serving individuals with ID promotes social interaction and the development of friendships, those friendships are far more likely to occur. In fact, it is highly likely that behavioral difficulties and monies spent on those difficulties will decrease as friendships increase.

Martin Seligman (2011) wrote about the positive effects of friendship in his book *Flourish*. He reported high correlations between individuals who have a high number of positive relationships and resiliency. This correlation was also found among soldiers. The soldiers who reported the strongest friendships and highest number of positive relationships were most resistant to PTSD. Carter et al. (2011) found that soldiers who had social support had significantly less PTSD than those who did not. In particular, they found that the support from positive spousal relationships helped most significantly in their study of 193 soldiers.

People with ID are the same. They need friendships in order to strengthen resiliency. They need spouses or significant others and many friends to ward off the traumatic effects of many aspects of living with intellectual disability. Most importantly, they need the opportunity to form real, not paid relationships. According to Seligman (2011), this is a critical factor of human happiness in the human condition, and according to the Declaration of Independence, the right to purse happiness is an unalienable right for all human beings. The pursuit of relationships can be supported by staff and agencies or undermined, it all depends on focus, not finances.

References

Carter, S.,Loew, B., Allen, E., Stanley, S., Rhoades, G., & Markman, H. (2011). Relationships between soldiers with PTSD symptoms and spousal communication during deployment. *Journal of Traumatic Stress, 24,* 352–355.

Herman, J. (1997). *Trauma and recovery.* New York: Basic Books.

McLaughlin, P. J., & Wehman, P. (Eds.). (1992). *Developmental disabilities: A handbook for best practices.* Boston: Andover Medical Publishers.

Seligman, M. (2011). *Flourish.* New York: Free Press

Siegel, D. J. (2010). *The mindful therapist: A clinician's guide to mindsight and neural integration.* New York: W. W. Norton.

Wolfensberger, W. (2011). Social role valorization: A proposed new term for the Principle of Normalization. *Intellectual and Developmental Disabilities, 49,* 435–40.

12

Stepping into the Here and Now

Misplaced Control

What is really needed for recovery from trauma? Judith Herman (1997) asserted: "No intervention that takes power away from the survivor can possibly foster his or her recovery." By implementing behavior plans that put the onus of control of behavior into the hands of staff, we take the power away from the individual. Through the functional assessment, which is used to determine what the individual is attempting to gain through his or her behaviors, and through the procedures that instruct staff on how control behavioral outbursts and difficulties, we have given staff the message that they are in charge and responsible for the behaviors of the individual whom they are serving. Individuals are given the message that they are unable to control themselves and must have a behavior plan so that the staff can be instructed in how to assert control over them and their behaviors. Often, when there are behavioral problems, regardless of the implementation of the plan, staff are accused of not implementing the plan correctly. Thus, staff are blamed for not controlling the individual in an expert enough manner.

Very often staff are implementing their own plans behind closed doors. This is what many of us in the field refer to as "the unwritten plan." Individuals may be bullied in these situations or overly controlled. My experience has been that, if this is the case, the individual will often develop unpredictable explosive behaviors or make repeated attempts to run away. This is the only way to assert power for the individual who has been rendered powerless. This might be acceptable for parents and children (barely), but it is definitely no way for one adult to treat another adult.

In addition, the psychologist charges a great deal of money for designing the written plan, whether or not it is followed. That money, more often than not, is taken out of the money allotted for services to that particular individual. The result of that expense is that there is less money for recreation, vacations, and other activities that the individual might choose if given power over his or her own life. Many individuals do not have any power or say over any financial matters relating to them. Case managers, house managers, and even parents will all decide how allotted money is to be spent; rarely does the individual make the decision. And these are the people who decide that money should be spent on designing behavior plans to control that individual's behavior.

Most of us know that when someone else wants us to change and tells us how much we should change and tries to manipulate or trick us into changing, we usually resist. For those of us who are married and who have tried to change the behavior of our spouses in some way or another, we are likely to be familiar with the ways in which adult humans resist change that is forced upon them. Adults with ID are no different. They want their power back. They want input. They want to direct the course of their life in some manner that feels real to them, not fake, as in a group of people sitting around a table congratulating themselves on giving an individual with ID some token choice and yet still determining the course of his or her life.

I would feel hopeless and traumatized if other people determined the course of my life. I would feel like a child in an adult's body. I would also feel alone. I am sure that many individuals with ID feel this way and resent services that they are given as a result. We may say that they are going through an "adolescent phase." I have even said this at times. But I was wrong. On a physical and emotional level, they are adults. Adults with souls. There is an awareness that is deeper than we often realize. And there is pain as well.

EMDR and ID

A very exciting study is currently under way in which adults with intellectual disability are receiving EMDR as a form of therapy. Doctoral candidate Lynn Buhler (2011) is conducting research for her dissertation about individuals with ID who have trauma. She is systematically using EMDR with them to address both single and complex trauma events and correlative PTSD symptoms. After extensive review of a variety of treatment modalities, she has concluded that EMDR would have the most promising application for individuals with ID. As I have been using this form of therapy for over 10 years, I certainly agree. EMDR is a highly effective tool when conducting therapy with individuals with ID.

Joseph

I recently worked with someone who was referred to me because he was engaging in many power struggles with staff and defying staff wishes at every turn. I recommended that we do therapy instead of a behavioral intervention initially. Joseph was deaf, and not much was known about his history. He had been in the agency where I worked for several years. There were no problems with him until his hours of supervision were increased and staff were told that they had to help and guide him more directly. All Joseph ever told us was that he was better off without the staff. When staff walked with Joseph in the community, Joseph made loud noises. The staff member would become upset when people turned and stared at them. Staff wanted me to get Joseph to stop this.

As I dug and talked with Joseph, his feelings of resentment came out. "I am an adult!" he signed to us. "I don't need these people!" Finally, Joseph started to describe a horrible bike accident that he had been in. He had been knocked unconscious and badly hurt when he had been hit by a truck while biking on a street. Joseph revealed that he had loved to bike many places. He had regularly biked 2 hr to the beach. He had had a great deal of independence through the use of his bike for many years. Now he was afraid to use his bike. He described flashbacks in which he would remember his accident and what it felt like waking up in the hospital in terrible pain. He said he was afraid to ride his bike again. I asked Joseph whether he would like to engage in EMDR in order to directly address the effects of this single trauma. Joseph agreed.

Staff joined us the day of the first EMDR session. We worked, using the protocol developed by Francine Shapiro (2001) for addressing single trauma events. By the end of the first session, the accident had gone from being highly disturbing to Joseph to being only mildly disturbing: 3 on a scale of 1 to 10. The following week, Joseph came back eagerly to continue working on his trauma. We did EMDR again (it should be noted that I have the appropriate training and certification from the EMDR organization for this work). The accident went from disturbing Joseph on a level of 3 out of 10 to a level of 0. Then he turned to the staff member present and asked for assistance in getting a bike.

Was this staff person happy? No. This person turned to me and said, " Great! Now Joseph is going to run away!" Evidently the staff did sense that Joseph had wanderlust. Joseph also wanted and needed control over his life. I encouraged the staff to get Joseph a bike. They resisted, and I increased my advocacy efforts. In the meantime, Joseph did run away, without a bike. He might have gone to look for one. I reassured staff that he would be back. He did return after a few days.

Joseph later told us that he had spent much of his life living like a hobo until he was picked up for services by the disability system. Joseph did have one staff person who would take him places and knew to act in the community as though they were friends. Another staff member, however, was very aware of the staff–client power relationship and wanted it to be clear, when in the community, that she was in charge of Joseph. This is the more traditional model, which sets up a nonnegotiable power differential in the community. Because Joseph was afraid of riding his bike, he felt dependent on this staff person. He demonstrated his dislike of this dependency and his despondency at the loss of freedom through his refusal to obey her many directions. They were in a standoff.

The EMDR gave Joseph his power back. It worked in a very specific manner on a very specific trauma event and associated emotions. Joseph felt empowered, even before he got his bike. He now does have a bike and takes regular bike trips with a much better helmet.

Cognitive Behavioral Therapy

A respected psychologist recently wrote in a 2009 textbook, "Cognitive restructuring may not be appropriate for clients demonstrating psychosis or mental deficits (e.g., autism, mental retardation)." As someone who has used cognitive restructuring and other cognitive behavioral techniques for over 20 years with individuals with ID, I was offended. When I began in the field, many people told me that I could not do therapy with "these people." That assessment was so very wrong. Cognitive restructuring is actually highly effective when the therapist does it on the appropriate cognitive level.

One technique that I developed for individuals who have experienced a great deal of trauma takes the following approach: First, the individual tells his or her story to the therapist. As any therapist knows, this may take a long time and a great deal of trust building. Then the therapist retells that story. In the retelling, the story becomes an epic tale, and the individual takes on the role of a great hero—much like *The Odyssey*, with the individual with ID cast as the great Odysseus. To tell individuals their story back to them and reframe it for them with them as a hero, which they are, is highly effective in restructuring the view of self. Then the therapist must reinforce this again and again. Another way to reinforce this is through the workbook that I developed, *My Book About Recovery!* (Harvey, 2009). I wrote a book for therapists describing many techniques and workbooks that I have come up with as a guideline for effective therapy. There are also wonderful books written and published by NADD Press on the same topic. Many therapists are actually doing therapy and adapting cognitive behavioral techniques to individuals with ID (Fletcher, 2010).

If therapy were the topic of this book, I would elaborate on more techniques and approaches that could be used by mental health professionals when working with individuals with ID. Instead, I would like to encourage providers to use the mental health professionals available to them to and to have confidence that these professionals can and should take a therapeutic approach to the treatment of individuals with ID who have trauma.

Conditions for Treatment

Conditions for treatment should include conditions of the recovery triangle described in Chapter 11. Treatment does not work if an individual is not safe or does not feel safe. Treatment is effective and recovery can begin only if the individual is in a situation in which he or she feels safe. That means safe staff, safe workplace, safe home. Unless the individual is feeling safe, recovery cannot begin. Even if the program assesses the individual as safe, but the individual does not feel safe, recovery cannot begin.

If the individual is alienated and isolated from others, treatment must involve reconnecting that person, in a way that is comfortable for that person, to others. Trauma cannot be addressed until individuals feel connected to others in their life. And, as stated before, if individuals do not perceive themselves as having any power over their life, recovery cannot occur. A powerless person does not have the hope, energy, or internal resources to do the therapeutic work involved in recovery from trauma. This person must have the ability to make real, not fake choices in his or her life and the ability to affect others on some level. Invisible people do not recover.

Stepping Into the Here and Now

Our task as a community is to help the individual with ID who is suffering from trauma to engage in the recovery process. We have to set the stage for recovery by ensuring safety, empowerment, and connection. We have to engage the mental health professional, psychologists, social workers, and licensed master's-level psychologists in the therapeutic process. Behavior plans are not enough. The wrong plan is not only not enough—it soon becomes a road block to recovery. Right now the mental health professionals in the field of ID have to look seriously at adopting and adapting evidence-based treatment approaches for use with people with ID. These individuals can and do benefit from therapy. We have to work a little harder to train and engage therapists to courageously conduct that therapy. We have no choice.

If we want people with ID to be able to lead rich and fulfilling lives, we have to address the trauma that has been in their lives since the day they walked into their kindergarten class and were told they belonged somewhere else. We have to go back even further in the lives of those who were sexually, physically, or emotionally abused merely because they were in the wrong place at the wrong time with a disability. We have to go back even further for those who were traumatized physically in the womb as their keepers ingested cocaine, alcohol, and a variety of other substances that came their way. We must address the many levels of trauma endured by the very brave individuals with ID if we ever want to assist in their recovery.

We must understand that behaviors are actions and actions have reasons. Trauma is acted out every day. Individuals with ID are not trying to manipulate their environment for some desired outcome; they are expressing the accumulated effects of years of loss, rejection, and exclusion. It is time that, as a community, we face the trauma that the people we serve have endured and begin to treat it programmatically, therapeutically, and humanistically.

If we were in their shoes, what kind of services, treatment approach, and behavioral interventions would we wish someone to use? I challenge you to find the answer to that question and use it.

References

Buhler, B. (2011). *Effectiveness of therapy for adults with psychotherapy.* Unpublished doctoral dissertation.

Fletcher, R. (2010). *Psychotherapy with individuals with intellectual disabilities.* Kingston, NY: NADD Press.

Harvey, K. (2009). *My book about recovery!* Available at http://pid.thenadd.org/My%20 Book%20About%20Recovery.pdf

Herman, J. (1997). *Trauma and recovery.* New York: Basic Books.

Shapiro, F. (2001). *Eye movement desensitization and reprocessing (EDMR): Basic principles, protocols, and procedures.* New York: Guilford Press.

Date Due